SPINNERS, SPOONS AND WOBBLED BAITS

Companion volume by the same authors

Plugs and plug fishing

Spinners, spoons and wobbled baits

Barrie Rickards

and

Ken Whitehead

With contributions on game fishing by
Dave Steuart and Fred Taylor

with 60 photographs
and 17 diagrams

Adam and Charles Black
London

First published 1977
A. & C. Black Ltd
London WC1R 4JH

Rickards, Barrie
Spinners, spoons and wobbled baits.
1. Spin-fishing
I. Title II. Whitehead, Kenneth E
799.1'2 SH456.5

ISBN 0-7136-1798-5

Type set by The Humble Wordsmith Limited
187 High Street
Tonbridge, Kent, TN9 1BB

Contents

Acknowledgements

Since *Plugs and plug fishing* was published it seems that even more people have been prepared to assist us with the technicalities of producing *Spinners, spoons and wobbled baits,* which must surely reflect something nice about someone. Again, Tony Perrin of Abu helped greatly, as did John Hennes of Shakespeares and Henri Limouzin and Mepps of France. Jack Simpson, Clive Young and Les Beacroft allowed us the freedom of their shops, and we thank Vic Gibson and Dennis Howell at Dons of Edmonton for their help in making what is not normally available over the counter. Ron Coleby traced some necessary books that we needed; David Bursill made good prints from our at times dubious negatives. Nigel Swift of the R.A.F. School of Photography gave similar help and advice.

The final shaping of the typescript would not have been possible without the help of Christine Rickards at the keyboard and Phil Harris at the editorial desk. Finally, we should like to thank most warmly our many angler friends who have put up with out ceaseless chatter, made helpful suggestions, and have declared that they do not *really* mind Ken's jokes or Barrie's drawings.

Foreword

The subject of using artificial baits for pike and salmon is a topic that has been covered by writers for centuries (though, perhaps, less well understood by anglers in the past), but their value with other freshwater fish, especially perch, zander and — to a much lesser extent — chub, is something about which little has been written. So it is a particular pleasure to welcome this book from Barrie Rickards and Ken Whitehead, the second of their joint-productions written entirely for the 'spin-fisherman'.

Pike fishermen of long-standing may mistakenly regard the authors as primarily natural-bait fishermen. But as their first work, *Plugs and plug fishing,* showed most admirably, their practical knowledge of other aspects of angling for British predatory fish is, to say the least, extensive. To achieve their measure of consistent success throughout the year, especially with pike, is a clear indication of their intimate understanding of all the approaches on waters of every nature. Happily for us, their skills and experience are matched by an ability to convey knowledge to others, which they do with zest and good humour.

To make the very best of this considerable depth of experience *Spinners, spoons and wobbled baits* should be read alongside the authors' book on plugs, for the two make what is undoubtedly a unique contribution to our angling literature. Furthermore, the scope of this latest book is broadened by the excellent chapters on salmon and trout by Dave Steuart and Fred Taylor. It would be difficult to imagine a more comprehensive coverage.

The privilege of a pre-production examination of the manuscript of this work, coupled with the knowledge gained from reading *Plugs and plug fishing,* encourages me to recommend Barrie and Ken's new book to all members of the great angling fraternity. None will fail to learn from it; all will gain pleasure from the obvious enthusiasm of the writers.

Martin Gay
March 1977

Introduction

Spinning is one of the first ways we get into a big fish or two when youngsters: a definite step up from snatching small roach and gudgeon on tiny hooks, is to set up a bar-spoon and catch half-pound perch, small trout or a jack pike or two. When Barrie equipped his six-year-old son Jeremy with a five-foot rod, bought from Percy Anderson; a ten-pound b.s. line; a Veltic bar-spoon and a 4-inch Russian 'Jim Vincent', he promptly caught several small perch, a $6\frac{3}{4}$ lb carp, and a $10\frac{1}{4}$ lb pike, all in a week! Spinners are cheaper and easier to make than plugs, so the youngster tends to stick with them for a long time, in the process learning a lot about casting skill and accuracy: any fool can throw a plug a long way, but casting spinners and spoons is about midway in delicacy between plugging and the roach-fishing tackle he probably began with. And spinning stays with you as a deadly and enjoyable technique.

Now we do not want to suggest that any angler goes out for the day armed only with spinners: he'll probably have plugs as well. Incidentally the opposite does obtain, since it is common enough to come across plug fanatics with no spinners in their bag. Often, when a particular fish is difficult we have found plugs to be more effective than spinners, but quite commonly the use of plugs puts the fish down and a small, twinkling spinner will succeed. On yet other days pike and trout in particular will completely ignore plugs and snap up spinners one after another. Quite recently (Dec. 1976) Barrie shared a bag of twenty-six pike with his companion Tony Legge, and of the nineteen fish taken by Barrie, fifteen fell to Ondex spinners (seven in one swim, and four on successive casts) whilst plugs were completely ignored. Similarly, it is not unusual to find trout go off small Plucky Bait type plugs as the water fines down after a flood, and yet they will take quill minnows, mackerel spinners or Mepps with great abandon.

You will have noticed that the above pike catch, a not inconsiderable one, was made in the winter, and whilst it is true that artificial baits score less well as a general rule during the winter months, there are plenty of exceptions for the enthusiast and, more importantly, there are waters in all regions which respond to artificials in winter. In one afternoon recently Les Beacroft and Barrie had nineteen good pike to artificials (plugs and spoons in this case) and only one to a natural bait.

What we are trying to say is that whilst spinners and spoons are often at the bottom of the list for winter pike men, they *can* be extremely effective, and in the summer are often superlative. For trout we've often thought spinners to be more effective than plugs, and for salmon — well, let's ask Dave Steuart to tell us in Chapter 15.

The scope of this book about the disease of spinning includes most aspects of fresh water spinning. Fred J. Taylor pens a highly original chapter on spinning for trout, and Dave Steuart is his inimitable self in spinning for salmon and sea-trout. We wrote a book called *Plugs and plug fishing* in 1976, and this present tome is intended to be largely *complementary* to that book. In other words, we shall not repeat the section on echo-sounding, pertinent though it is to any spinning fanatic, nor will we repeat ourselves on some other matters such as miscellaneous tackle. But we have considered again some questions of rods, reels and landing equipment, and tackle boxes, since there have been some improvements recently and some additional thoughts from us. Occasionally, where we think it will be helpful, we refer to the earlier book so that the reader can cross refer if he or she wishes.

Sea spinning is a topic in its own right, and whilst we couldn't fail to have been excited over the years by writers of the calibre of Hugh Stoker and Derek Fletcher, our experience of spinning at sea is limited and the subject vast. We would recommend the reader to search out some of the discourses on baited spoon techniques for flounders, for this is a technique we are certain will catch on in fresh water.

Whilst on the subject of natural baits we have included a section on *spun* deadbaits, as on Archer flights, and also on wobbled deadbaits. Both techniques are half-way to what one might term 'pure' bait fishing methods, particularly the latter, but the essence of both techniques is movement along a more or less linear track and attraction by flash and movement.

In the text we often refer to named items of tackle. These are the ones we personally use and have found to be effective. We do not imply that others are not as good: there are, for example, dozens of high quality reels on the market today. The same applies to lures. When we wrote *Plugs and plug fishing* some anglers wanted to know why we recommended surface poppers and crawlers for use in British waters.

We did so because we had found them *to be highly successful* with perch and pike. Similarly, the spinners recommended in this book are *extremely good;* if they are not, then we say so. Again, there must be many spinners we haven't tried, and we do not wish to denigrate these at all. There is tremendous scope for experiment on the part of the individual angler. As a matter of fact, nowhere is this better seen than when the angler makes his own spinners and spoons. We deal with this at some length in Chapter 7, but suffice it to say that making and painting spoons is one of the real delights of angling since it requires little or no technical skill. With those remarks we shall let you loose on the rest of the book.

PART ONE

Tackle

1

Rods

There are not many anglers who do not possess a spinning rod. At least, when they are asked if they spin they readily admit to it, but fail to add that the spinning rod also doubles for various forms of legering and swingtip work, with a little deadbaiting thrown in if they want an extra rod at some time. In short, they own a multipurpose rod with which they spin.

Can they really spin with it? In theory, yes, and in practice the rod can be made to; after all, it is possible to play billiards with a rolled umbrella for a cue, as one world champion has demonstrated. But the difference between chuck and chance it with any old rod and consistent results with a well balanced outfit is in pleasure and relaxation, the very roots on which angling is founded.

The big mistake made by many beginners (and some experts) in spinning is in just wandering into a tackle shop and selecting a rod. By doing this the rod is merely purchased for the rod's sake — perhaps because the colour, appearance, or finish attracts the would-be purchaser, with little or no thought given to what the rod will do, or where it would be used.

We both think that before the purchase of a rod is even considered the angler would do better to sit down and analyse his fishing needs, appreciating that no one rod will cover every type of water and species of fish, but that a little forethought and planning can prevent the expense of a battery of rods purchased over the years until the right one or two are found. We did it the wrong way, as you'll have guessed.

So let us allow our imagination to run riot for a few minutes, and try to envisage some average spinning waters. Think first of a large river. To reach the area where a fish might lie, which is often against a far bank, is

1 Compactness: a Taiwanese telescopic rod and Shakespeare reel. Ready for immediate use.

going to require a fairly hefty bait and a strong line to carry it. Also the river may be fairly full, perhaps even in flood, in which case it may be necessary to add weight to the bait by some means or other to get it well down below the surface.

Now think big in another direction, and imagine a large lake, reservoir or loch. If it contains really big fish we may want to use a big bait. If boats are not allowed then we may want to cast that bait over very long distances to reach 'fishy' areas, or if a boat *is* allowed, then we may want to get a bait thirty or so feet below the surface to reach them. Again, we are thinking of heavy or big baits, added weight, and a strong line.

Turn now to the other extreme. Big rivers at times of very low water, small rivers without much flow, small streams, and lakes and ponds where casting over a long distance is of no great importance but accuracy may be. Certainly there is no case here for big baits and strong lines — rather the reverse; a situation calling for delicate baits and light lines that will not scare fish.

Has this flight of fancy produced anything useful? We think so. It acknowledges that weight of lure and strength of line are of prime importance in spinning. It also shows that size and strength of water are equally important, and in perspective proves that these facts dictate any sort of rod we may use. In short, water governs the weight, weight governs the line, and the rod is an accessory to spinning — never the reverse.

So if all our spinning is to be directed to big, powerful waters then a big, powerful rod will be required to get the bait to where it is wanted and manage the weight needed to keep it down at its fishing depth. The rod for this type of fishing will be referred to as double-handed. In other words, because of its size and weight two hands are required to use it, and the handle is made long enough for both of them to be used together. The handle may be up to 30 inches (76 cm) long.

Just how long should the rod be? Well, in theory the longer the rod the better its ability to cast over a long distance. But Cholmondely Pennell, writing in his *Book of the Pike* in 1865 mentions that the weight of a rod 18 feet long was 'trying', winning with it our Understatement of the Century award. Weight apart, another disadvantage of the over-long rod is that it is not very accurate, and whilst it may not be necessary to place a lure within a foot or two of an area in a big water, some control of accuracy can be a distinct advantage, even if it is only to repeat a previous cast. In general, accuracy with long rods cannot be achieved at the moment of setting the bait on its trajectory, but is better done by giving sufficient force on the cast to overcast, and then braking back the lure by trailing a finger on the reel spool. This way, only the direction of the cast has to be accurate.

In practice, 10 to 11 feet of rod is generally considered an ideal length for heavy spinning, providing that the rod has the right taper. Taper, the reduction in circumference from butt to tip, is all-important. It provides 'give' i.e. curve, which can help the cast by storing energy during the early part of the rod's forward movement and returning it as the bait is moving, helping to achieve distance. If the taper is mainly in the tip of the rod the acceleration of the bait wili be fast and accurate. However, there is a disadvantage in that acceleration applied in this way puts an enormous strain on both bait and line, giving every chance that either or both could break long before the cast is complete.

So the best action to select is one described as 'slow', meaning that the taper goes fairly evenly from butt to tip, allowing it to curve throughout its length during the cast. It certainly does not mean, as many anglers believe, that the rod is whippy. Were this the case then no distance of any sort would be achieved.

During recent years much has been written and heard of the reverse taper rod. In brief, this means that the rod tapers from the tip outwards to the reel fitting, then, through a long handle, it tapers back again to the butt cap. In theory, extra energy is stored during the build-up of the cast, to be unleashed at the moment of release. In practice that is so, but there is a tendency for the rod to continue to curve downwards after the cast, causing friction and deflecting the bait from its intended path. We feel that the added advantage of the reverse taper is grand for beach casters, where one could then use a rather lighter than usual rod, but of no enormous significance in a spinning rod.

The stepped-up rod, usually one which has received an extra wrapping of glass fibre cloth during the manufacturing stage, is stiffer than the ordinary rod, and capable of harder work and handling heavier baits. It is an excellent weapon where heavy deadbaits or big lures have to be flung over long distances.

Now let us think about those other waters we imagined where distance was not the object, but accuracy and delicacy the major factor. Obviously the long rod with its slow taper would be unnecessary, in fact the light line and small lure would produce such an imbalance that casting of any sort would be nearly impossible.

This is where the short rod, between 6 and 8 feet, is a necessity. Because it is small, it can be used single-handed, which in itself allows for better co-ordination of movement when the cast is made, and so improves accuracy. The action, or taper, should be fast, most of the spring taking place between the tip and mid-section of the rod itself. Used with a light line the bait can be accurately flicked over a short distance with the minimum of fatigue. In contrast to the long rod the bait is fired *at* the target.

One final definition should be mentioned before leaving this discussion on rod sizes, and that is balance. We have both seen anglers who, when asked if a rod was balanced, have placed it over a finger in an effort to show that with the reel mounted it balanced at a point just above the handle. Of course that is balance, but only a part of it. The more important point to remember is that balance must also refer to the outfit as a whole — lure, line and rod, in that order.

Naturally there can be mutations of grey in our rather black and white rod picture. There is the chap who wants to fish a small, deep and fast river and who decides that a slow action 'heavy' rod eight feet long is his answer; or the angler who fishes a small stream with heavy bankside herbage, so decides on a long, fast-tapered rod that will reach well out from the banks before the lure is flicked out. But they are applying the very first of our principles — that of considering the water and weight before deciding on the rod.

> '*If you spin long, weight talks. If you are not catching fish — weight shrieks'.* So wrote the late Edward Spence.

Having decided on the type of rod, consideration must next be given to the material from which it is constructed and various fittings that are essential. We feel that the quotation from Edward Spence gives the underlying message to the words that follow, remembering always that it is a fool's economy to sacrifice strength for weight.

Materials for rod construction now fall under two main categories — split cane and glass fibre. A few of the 'golden oldies' do exist — this season, Ken found a youngster on a Thames weirpool using a greenheart spinning rod for trout. Just watching the rod work was to appreciate how sweet its action was, but knowing how fickle greenheart can be and its potential for snapping like a rotten carrot, Ken found himself quietly praying that the boy didn't connect with a rod-bender whilst he was within earshot. We have both in recent seasons seen immediate post-war drawn steel rods in use with spinning outfits. In fact, if you listened hard enough you could hear the rattle of rust running about inside the tubes with every cast!

Split cane is not only very much in vogue in some circles but its use in general is on the increase. Old though the principles of its construction may be, modern glues and efficiency have made it more pleasing to use than ever, its light responsive touch in a rod providing a lot of satisfaction that makes a day's fishing. But its very expense is offputting to a large section of would-be purchasers. Yes, there is some cheap stuff around, but cheapness in split cane usually means that a sacrifice has been made somewhere along the production line — and cheapness means expense when a break occurs.

Hardy's, who make some of the best split cane in the world, demand around seventy 'green'uns' before they will part with a built cane spinning rod, and most of the big names are not many pounds behind them. We feel that we would want a lot of use from a rod for that type of money, and use is one of the things that one has to be careful with where split cane is concerned. It strains quite easily, taking on a pronounced 'set', or curve, which means re-whipping the rings on the reverse side of

2 An 'antique' catch. 1910 Hardy Victor rod, Silex reel, silk line, Pubjab steel trace and Hardy Wye Phantom. Taken on the River Lea.

the rod to effect a partial cure. Also, considerable care must be taken over storing when the rod is not in use, otherwise that dreaded set can strike again. In a nutshell, split cane is great for the purists and financiers of this world, but not for the bread-and-margarine lads like ourselves.

Which brings us to glass fibre, the most popular material in everyday use. Light (in its hollow form), and strong (but not enough to withstand slamming in a car door), it can be purchased in nearly every shape and size imaginable. Rods made from solid blanks are available, carrying more weight than the hollow counterparts, and are grand for really tough work where great strains have to be exerted when tackle becomes snagged. Unfortunately, most solid glass rods are ruined by big, heavy ferrules that completely spoil the balance.

Hollow tubes are usually joined by means of a spigot, hollow in itself or solid, shedding weight and providing extra toughness at an acknowledged weak point of the rod. Some are now made with carbon-reinforced sections, compensating for wear and adding even more strength. Beware of bad fitting during the manufacturing stage though, and carefully check the rod by putting the joints together and feeling for 'sloppiness' before actually buying.

This section would not be complete without mention of carbon fibre rods which are gradually appearing on the rod stands. A few spinning rods have been made available in this material, and although we have not had the chance to try them, we have both handled fly rods made from the same material.

Certainly the lightness of these rods is outstanding, and their ability to cope with various line weights is quite extraordinary. But it is an innovation and we feel that there could well be a few bugs and gremlins that have yet to be eliminated. Price-wise it is in the built cane bracket, and all things considered we have decided to wait a few years yet before thinking of reviewing or ousting our glass fibre favourites. By that time production and price may present a different picture.

The handle on a spinning rod is something accepted without comment by the majority of anglers, but we both reckon that this is the most intimate part of the instrument. Comfort here will influence not only casting, but to a lesser degree one's whole concentration during the day.

Cork is the usual handle material, and there is no doubt that good quality solid cork is warm, comfortable, clean and long-lasting. We are emphatic that the circumference of the corks should suit our hands, long experience having taught us that thin handles lead to sloppy casting and over-thick grips become tiring. For most adult males a diameter of about 1 inch (2.5 cm) is about right. We also dislike sudden ridges or tapers up and down the corks, and abhor short two-handed rod handles that make us pigeon-chested when gripping them with both hands spread in the casting position.

Sheet cork handles are usually thin cork wound round a wooden former. Modern ribbed plastic, and wooden handles, rate rather low in our opinion, usually because of the 'cold' touch. Some leather-wound handles are great, providing that the diameter of the blank is sufficient to make a comfortable grip. But in recent months Fuji of Japan have marketed an entirely new concept in handles with their Fujispeed Grip (see Photo. 3).

Made from plastic, with an imitation leather finish, the Fujispeed Grip does away with reel mountings in any form. The handle unscrews into two parts, the reel is inserted, and then the halves are screwed together again. Simple, safe and foolproof. There are numbers of collets which fit inside the handle end, enabling any diameter of blank to be fitted. Ken has only seen one in the single-handed size, but feels it to be a warm, comfortable winner.

It is generally accepted that handles on spinning rods should be parallel for fixed spool reels, and cranked for multipliers. But there is much to recommend a cranked handle with a closed face reel, because it tends to iron out the kink between line exit on the reel and the first rod ring. Again, a matter of preference and, of course, deciding on what type of fishing one intends to do before selecting the rod.

Rod fittings we regard as a necessary evil. Those rods with screw-winch fittings have the reel position fixed: not always a good thing. The alternative is sliding fittings that have a nasty habit of coming apart and dropping the reel at one's feet during the day, to the detriment of fish, fishing and fisherman.

Every man to his taste: Ken belongs to the belt and braces brigade and favours screw fittings for safety, whilst Barrie is happy with his push fittings. Ken has, however, moderated his views in recent months after trying the Fuji sliding fittings made from very strong, pliable plastic. Not only are they light, but they lock up on to the reel saddle and seem less prone to slip than the chrome counterparts.

One last type of reel fitting is worth considering, and this is the whip-on locking fittings. Certainly nothing could be lighter and the position can always be moved, albeit with a little trouble. Where lightness — and that is the theme of this section — is required, then this fitting with leather hand-grips takes first place.

This leaves only rod rings. In a manufacturer's trade catalogue you will find dozens of types listed, but only a few of them appear on rods in the shops. Actually, we demand the impossible from rings by expecting them never to wear out. Fortunately, there are now some first-rate metal rings on the market, principally those made from Diamite. But good as these may be, they are likely to groove in a few seasons, wreaking havoc on any line drawn over them.

Once or twice a year we run the point of a pin around each ring on our rods. The slightest crack or groove will cause the point to catch, even

3 Fuji handles.

with marks hardly visible to the human eye. This is the signal that the ring needs replacing before the next outing and not after it. We then have a second check on our lines for possible wear despite the fact that they are always tested before we fish.

The size of leg on a ring is a personal preference, but generally short legs are the best for heavy lines, longer legs for fine lines likely to cling to the rod on a wet day. Lined rings with linings such as Sintox, Regalox, or Aqualite are heavier than the wire variety, can still wear, and are rather expensive. There is a tendency also for the weight to alter the action of the rod, making it softer, and we still apply our pin test just as regularly as with the metal varieties.

Several new lined rings have made an appearance on the market, one notable new design being those from (again!) Fuji, which are lightweight, have a lined centre and are mounted by one leg only. Whilst we have not had the chance to test the ring centre for wear over a couple of seasons, we find that mounting by one leg only saves a certain amount of stiffening of the rod action that naturally occurs when the two leg ring is used.

Perhaps the most important thing with rings is their spacing. Too few rings attached to a rod will lead to the line cutting at angles across the curve of the rod — and this means strain, friction, and line wear. Too many rings will stiffen the rod action (or if lined, soften it; and in any case increase weight) and lead to friction that can reduce the length of any cast made. Moral: run a line through the rod rings and bend the rod with it before making a final decision on which rod to buy. If it doesn't look right, then leave the rod alone, or plan carefully to re-ring it if you prefer the rod for other reasons.

Of course, it is difficult to find all that one imagines to be ideal in a spinning rod ready for purchase in a rod-pack. That is probably why more and more anglers are making their own rods, experimenting with various blanks, handles and fittings until they have just what they want for their type of fishing. The task is not difficult, the amount of money saved is often large, and the pleasure in the making enormous. Nor need the task be a headache to the all-thumbs handyman. When buying parts, any reputable tackle dealer will be only too pleased to offer free advice on rod building.

We offer no apologies that this chapter has contained some very elementary knowledge. It has been included not only for the beginner who is about to purchase his first rod but also as a 'thinking point' for the chap who has done a little spinning and is considering some serious work, as well as the expert looking for new ideas on which to experiment.

Remember that if you are spinning, the rod stops in your hand all day. You cannot, as the bottom fisherman does, set the rod aside in rests — not as a general rule, anyway. Something as personal as a spinning rod deserves thought and consideration before it is chosen.

2

Reels

Multiplying, centre pin, fixed spool, or closed face reel — which is the best one? Well, you pay your money and you take your choice, probably to discover a few sins and omissions at a later date. The trouble is, of course, that if you ask someone for advice he is sure to recommend his favourite, outlining all that is good and little or nothing that is bad. With today's prices experience is an expensive thing to buy, so we intend to set down the pro's and con's of each type of reel, unveiling a few shortcomings that are often implicitly accepted, but seldom openly acknowledged.

The multiplying reel is an improvement on the old centre pin reel that it resembles. Line is wound round a centre drum which is turned by a handle. In turning, the action is applied through a train of gears, multiplying the action of the drum so that it turns several times to one complete revolution of the handle. The whole thing can be thrown out of gear, i.e. the drive taken off the handle, in which case the drum turns on two very fine pivots, allowing line to run free with little or no resistance. This enables casts to be made straight off the reel over a considerable distance. Because there is difficulty in slowing the drum down to coincide with the end of the cast when the bait runs out of steam, there is often a set of governing pads (small washers mounted on rods) which are thrown outwards against the inside of the reel during motion, and act as a brake. The thumb can also be used as a most efficient brake.

Line pulls off the real straight up the rod rings (more especially where the cranked rod handle is used) so that there is only one angle where friction and wear can occur — and that is at the rod tip. By using various sizes the reel can handle very heavy baits and lines, and with a little sensible lubrication and care is long-lasting and relatively free of wear.

So much for the good news: now for the bad. Quite a lot of anglers would immediately list the price first. Fair crack — they are more expensive than the other types; but we feel that you can expect a lifetime's use out of your money and if you average that out over, say, only twenty years — it is a cheap buy. Another problem is that the fine spindles on which the drum revolves can bend and distort, giving some pretty odd casts before the damage is diagnosed. Well, this problem only occurs when considerable strain has been put on the drum of the reel via the line, invariably the result of pulling hard on a snagged lure or line to effect a break. Hardly ever, we regret to say, is this excessive strain caused by a big fish.

This is one of the problems you cure by prevention. In other words, never snatch or tug hard against the immovable; lay the rod down, wind the line above the rod tip around your arm several times then pull to free the lure. Win or lose, the price of a lure is insignificant compared to the damage that can be caused to an expensive reel.

Yet another problem one can encounter is with line sliding underneath preceding coils round the drum, so that in the middle of a stupendous cast, lure, lead and line fall around the angler's head — a situation in which only the vocabulary is improved. Cause? Pulling hard on the line again, forcing the coil immediately around the drum to bite under those below it. Remedy? Use the pulling-for-a-break technique previously explained if you become snagged.

But the two big drawbacks to this reel that really reduce its acceptance are the inability of an angler to master the art of casting with it, and the limitations of the reel in handling *really light lures.* We hinted at the first problem earlier with the free running spool that continues when the line and lure have stopped. This causes the line around the spool to churn up into an enormous ball — a bird's nest in fact — that takes hours to unravel, if it's worth bothering with at all.

However, when the reel is new there will be a sheet of instructions with it explaining how various parts can be adjusted so that overrunning can be avoided, and if they are followed then the problem practically disappears. But there is often a human element involved in angling disasters and some people never learn how to use the adjustments. In casting, the alternative to operating all the mechanical aids is to use a thumb to check the speed of the spool progressively as the cast nears its end. Again, this is something that takes practice to perfect and the apprenticeship can be a long and frustrating one. Many anglers never master it, and to find whether or not you fall into this category we strongly advise that before purchasing a multiplier you ingratiate yourself with the owner of such a reel in the hope of getting a demonstration, plus a few lessons. As a matter of fact, neither of us found multipliers too difficult and certainly neither of us would be without our multipliers which we use for heavy duty work, especially with large baits. They fit against the rod handle and, when a big fish is hooked, allow the angler to be complete master of the situation.

The inability to cast fine lines and lures (the natural inertia of the spool can only be overcome by weight) we accept, and one turns to another type of reel for this contingency.

Everybody is familiar with the fixed spool reel: indeed it is accepted without complaint and its faults are rarely mentioned. But it has some, not least that of acute line angles. And angles lead to friction, line wear, frustration and lost fish.

Line from the fixed spool leaves the drum and immediately travels at an angle of about 90° over the pick-up arm. Because the reel stands well proud of the handle there is another smaller angle, possibly 20°, as the line travels up to the rod rings, then over another 90° angle at the rod tip. More angles than with the multiplier and, of course, one big source of wear at the angle over the pick-up.

Most manufacturers acknowledge this weak point and may provide a roller bearing to prevent line cutting grooves in the metal. It is fair to say that many anglers never think of checking this bearing to ensure that it is moving and free of grit. Nor do they think of providing it with a little fine grease or oil to enable it to function more efficiently. Be warned!

One of the supposed delights of the fixed spool reel is the slipping clutch mechanism, the means by which a running fish can pull line from the reel without causing a break. Angling books and magazines have stressed the weakness of this mechanism for years; the nasty truth is that if you continue winding against a solid resistance the slipping clutch will allow the line to be turned, even though the spool is still, forcing a multitude of line twists that will cause havoc with future casts. But despite the publicity we still see dozens of anglers who wouldn't think of winding against a running fish merrily winding away when they are snagged! It is not a fish that provides the twisting, merely the revolving of the pick-up arm.

Richard Walker spoke a mountain of truth over clutch mechanisms when he hinted that, in playing a fish, the fine line and slipping clutch were a fallacy; if the water was clear they were unnecessary, and if it was

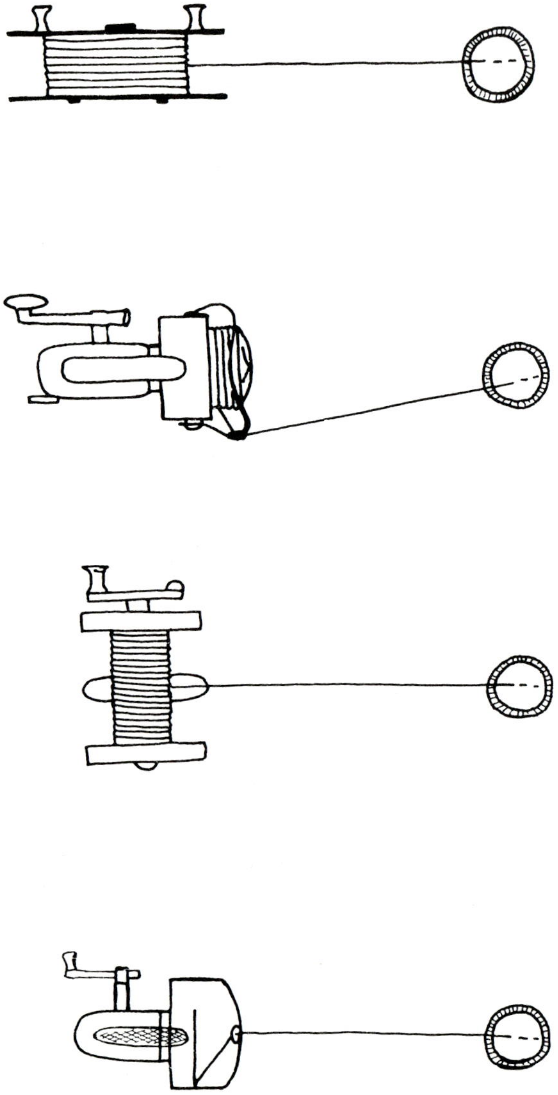

Fig. **A**

weedy they were useless — the line would snag, the fish could not be stopped and would break free. Partly because of this we tend to keep any slipping clutch we use bottled fairly tight, preferring to play a fish by using the handle. We also keep them that way because we frequently fail to keep a finger on the spool when striking — and a finely set clutch means that the spool will slip and fail to set the hooks home.

Fiddling with a reel whilst fishing is one of the most frustrating of exercises. One can get a certain amount of fiddle when adjusting the tension on a clutch because the drag button is in front of the reel, something very difficult for cold fingers to manoeuvre. The Abu style of adjustment, with the knob at the back of the gear frame, is grand and the numbered positions which indicate the various pressures are a great help when a line is changed.

The other line twisting, cutting, cursing fiddle is when line slips between the spool and its housing, to disappear in a maze of turns around the central spindle. Fortunately, several companies have produced the skirted reel, an extension of the spool which fits back over and not into the housing, making this problem almost obsolete.

Despite our list of problems which can arise with fixed spool reels, we like them, and for the considerable chunk of our middle to light range of spinning use nothing else, our ownership including those by Mitchell, Abu, Intrepid and, more recently, skirted reels by Diawa, Ryobi and Shakespeare. But always remember that these reels are not miracle machines and we make a point of stripping, examining, cleaning and oiling the several makes two or three times a year. Prevention is better than all the curses let loose over a lost fish.

Confession is good for the soul, so we list here the howlers we make when using the fixed spool reel, starting with the long distance cast driven off from the reel without having first opened the bail arm, usually followed by the equally famous cast made when a swivel has been wound up past the top ring of the rod. Both humiliations acceptable without bystanders, but very destroying to one's ego if half a dozen heads pop up along the bank wondering where the splash has come from. The correct call under these circumstances is 'Rising short'.

Attempting to play a fish from the handle with the anti-reverse latch on can cause one to consider wearing brown corduroy trousers for future outings. We try to leave ours off (anti-reverse latches, not the trousers) and have noticed that any occasional lapses all occurred after a reel maintenance session. Yet another gala performance can be guaranteed if a loop of line inadvertently becomes wound round the spool. The snatch this causes during a cast is referred to as a 'fifty-pencer' if the lure whips off. It will probably alter with inflation. If this happens line has become badly twisted, so play it off the spool down-stream from a bridge, or walk round a field towing it behind you. Otherwise the line will loop again.

Finally, a word on casting. After opening the bail arm, trap the line against the rim of the spool or better still hang it on the first or second finger, but not under your finger against the rod handle. A small point, but one that has a considerable effect on accuracy.

Our progression through the pro's and con's of various fishing reels has always started with the problem of the line angle, simply because this is one of the biggest line strain factors, and often the reason behind a sudden break that loses a fish.

With a closed face reel, basically a fixed spool design with the face covered by a metal hood, the problem of line angle becomes acute. Line leaves the spool and travels up and over its rim at an angle of nearly 180° until it appears through the mouth of the cover, to double back at an angle of approximately 20° up through the first rod ring (unless a cranked handle is being used) and eventually back over 90° at the tip ring (see Fig. A on page 16).

This creates one hell of a lot of friction and strain which is felt immediately anything heavy is played and, since one invariably uses a fine line on this type of reel, this is a constant source of weakening easily overlooked by the unwary. We are not condemning the closed face job — it is excellent for short distance casting on tight waters, where you may be faced with a cast between bushes where line can readily catch, and perfect for open waters on a windy day because line just cannot snag around the handle or body of the reel. It is all a question of keeping a mental awareness that one cannot use brute force.

Notice we said *short* casts. Because of its construction the spool of this reel is exceptionally narrow. Therefore line quickly runs down to a point where friction starts to affect its free running capacity over the lip of the spool, reducing casting distance.

Possibly the biggest danger with the closed face reel is in allowing line to snatch when playing a good fish, usually during the 'pumping' stages. The angler holds the handle firmly, pumps backwards with the rod on the fish — and then starts to wind down, lowering the rod tip to recover line. Because the various line angles we have already discussed cause friction and make turning the handle hard work, there is a risk that the angler will drop the rod tip quickly, recovering line without pressure against the fish. It is exactly at this moment, when the fish feels no resist-

4 Barrie punching a deadbait on a gravel pit.

ance, that he will make a lunge for freedom and the resulting snatch on the tightening line will be disastrous.

So our closed face reels are reserved for superlight fishing — the subject of a later chapter — when we anticipate that smaller fish will be caught under very sporting circumstances. But one cannot govern the size of fish one catches, and every now and again a heavyweight turns up. Great fun — providing one remembers the limitations of the reel.

Two other variations on the fixed spool reel are worthy of comment. First, the Mitchell Match reels with automatic pick-ups. It is not necessary to take off the pick-up before casting, but merely to hold it down with the index finger of the hand over the reel. On casting, you lift your finger at the precise moment, and the pick-up flies open. This reel was originally designed for match fishing but is excellent for spinning and more versatile than the closed face reel.

Second, the J. C. Higgins Spin-Casting reel (Photo. 5). This is a closed face reel which gets around the problem of deep, narrow spools, just mentioned in connection with usual closed face reels, by having a series of steps in the spool so that a relatively small amount of line is held on each step. This reel is unusual in several other respects: the cast is made with a finger on a button at the rear of the reel, which has the effect of trapping the line; the stepped spool is at the *back* of the flier housing, not at the front as with most other fixed spool and closed face reels. Sears, Roebuck and Co. made this reel and we hope they still do, for it seems to combine the advantages, for light spinning anyway, of both the fixed spool and closed face types.

We cannot close a chapter on spinning reels without a passing mention of the centre pin. Fundamentally, we have in this reel perfection. One line angle from drum to butt ring; one angle at the rod tip; no gears, spreaders, nor as a rule clutches or elaborate governing mechanisms. A

5 The J. C. Higgins (closed face) spin casting reel with stepped/reverse spool.

heave of the rod, the bait flies out, the drum is braked by a thumb as the cast ends; nothing could be simpler — at least in theory.

In practice, casting from the drum is one of the most difficult things to do, with the niceties of starting the drum in motion at the commencement of the cast and braking it down at the end requiring a sense of timing and touch that takes years to perfect. But some people do it, and grand it is to watch. Dave Steuart, who writes the chapter in this book on spinning for salmon and sea trout, is a renowned expert at use of the centre pin in all forms of fishing. Barrie also learned to master the art but, unlike cycling, it is an art lost without plenty of practice.

A good centre pin casting reel is now antique, and such reels fetch fairly high prices. But they are worth every penny, if only to admire the engineering work that would cost a fortune to produce today. Ken has a Hardy Silex, complete with drag and cutaway rim section further to assist thumb braking on the drum. Occasionally he uses it, but the pain from knuckles bruised by the rapidly spinning handles has stopped him really getting a grip on the style. It is all a matter of choice, and we tend to plump for the easy way every time.

Our final words on reels concern hands. Useful things to have when you fish — but never considered by a large section of the fishing fraternity. Now, one of your two hands is a 'master'. This is the hand you will use to hold a rod when casting, or playing a fish. Trouble is that quite a large number of people continue this master situation to the reel, choosing to use the master hand for turning the handle as well.

The result is a 'cross-hands boogie' as the angler constantly changes the rod from left to right hand and *vice versa*. The answer to the problem is to use the master for rod holding, and to train oneself to use the other hand for reel work. All very simple, but the majority of right-handed anglers purchase a reel on which the handles are set on the right-hand side, falling into a trap from which it is impossible to escape. One famous firm makes almost all its multipliers for left-handed anglers and its other reels for right-handed anglers!

Where the right hand is the master, then buy a left-handed reel, and *vice versa*. Many manufacturers make left- and right-hand wind as an option; in some cases the handle can be transferred from one side to the other. Believe us when we say that there are enough things to concentrate on if one is to spin successfully without being involved in constant hand-changing.

3

Lines, nets and gaffs

MONOFILAMENT

If you are considering spinning as a full-time sport then we suggest you read this chapter twice. If you are already well advanced in the craft, then we ask you to forget your Tooty Fruity Never Fail Nylon that you swear by, read with an open mind what follows and then reconsider your favourite again.

Did you hear the story of the spin-fisherman who decided to buy a 5 lb b.s. line? When he used it, he tied a bad knot, losing 40 per cent of its strength. At his first cast the line naturally became wet — and another 15 per cent of its strength was lost. Because he had a cracked rod ring the line frayed, and lost a further 20 per cent strength. By exposing it to the sun, stretching it when he became snagged, and keeping it in a warm cupboard it lost another 30 per cent. Next time he took his reel out of its case he found the line had disintegrated into a pile of dust!

Far fetched? A little — but not as far as you would think. Nylon may be better than horse hair, silk, flax, gutta percha, and all the other old fashioned trouble-makers of the past. But it is not a miracle material, and one needs to use a little thought before blindly purchasing it.

Let's start with two cast-iron, irrefutable facts. The *first* knot you tie in a nylon line reduces its strength by about 15 per cent if it is a good knot; up to 30 per cent or more if it is bad, or badly tied. We use the double clinch knot, or half blood knot, and take our time tying it. Before we ease it up tight (as opposed to pulling or jerking it) we moisten the loose knot in our mouths so that it won't 'strangle', and further reduce the line circumference. Tie more than one knot, and down sinks the strength of the line again — unless all the knots are as good or better than the first, in which case the theoretical loss (after the first knot) is nil.

Our other fact is that all nylon line, on becoming wet, loses up to 15 per cent of strength immediately. Which rather makes a mockery of our 5 lb line that we purchased — its actual breaking strain in use would be under 4 lbs. Of course, it is difficult to guard against ultra violet rays when one is fishing, but it is possible to use a little sense in purchasing line, and if it has been standing out in a showcase near a window, then look elsewhere.

Cracked rod rings we have dealt with in a previous section, likewise the problem of line angles on a reel, all of which produce friction, which in turn generates heat that destroys the properties of monofilament. But pulling and stretching a line? Obviously one cannot use a line without some strain. It is just a question of reducing it where possible, and being prepared to scrap lines at regular intervals and respool afresh.

We purchase our line in bulk spools, giving us the advantages of keeping it under ideal conditions, and being able to fill a spool or drum right to the brim. This is much better than spooling on the 100 metres or so, and then 'topping-up' with backing, only to be faced with rewinding the line so that the backing is next to the spool centre. Even though the line is new, we still run it carefully through our fingers as we wind on because flat (weak) spots are not unknown.

Which make is best? We plump for pliable, low glint lines and among those that we use are Maxima, Intrepid Superline, Sylcast and Platil. Although it is possible to further reduce glint by staining or dying, it may detract from the original strength and we prefer to leave the line in its original colour. Superline colours extremely well with Dylon dyes, and that which we dyed in 1975-76 is still sound.

BRAIDED LINES

On the credit side, braided lines made from nylon or dacron are softer and more pliable than monofilament, and less prone to lose strength when wet. They knot easily (but still, of course, lose strength with each knot tied) and are practically uninfluenced by the stretch factor that weakens most monofilament lines.

On the debit side they are not as long-lasting as monofilament and more prone to abrasions. There is a certain tendency to cling when wound round a drum, and by virtue of thickness alone create more friction when leaving the reel, lessening the distance that can be covered. Our main dislike is that they are very visible in clear water conditions, so much so that a nylon trace of some sort must be adopted for general use. As we have discovered, this means knots (in the plural) and subsequent loss of overall strength again. To sum up, braided lines are in a class of their own for trolling, but for us it is monofilament with all our general spinning work.

The exit line (Ye Gods! Where do they think of 'em?) in this section is on fitting line on to spools. Underfill a multiplying or fixed spool reel, and you are losing efficiency through friction. Overfill, and with the multiplier you create friction against the side plates of the frame; with the fixed spool reel you invite innumerable loops and tangles as line coils off the spool. Fill correctly, check frequently and renew regularly — these are our golden rules.

6 Quick release for the landing net with a dog-lead clip.

NETS

When we wrote *Plugs and plug fishing,* Ken indulged in a long paragraph describing his perfect landing net. By any stretch of imagination his main request for a full sized net that would fold to pocket handkerchief size would be impossible to produce. By the same token it would also be impossible to produce our most recent brain child to help solve the landing situation — one with legs that could follow behind the angler. But our imaginary thoughts do highlight the number one problem that centres around a decent net; the fact that somehow, somewhere, it has to be carried unobtrusively, but always ready.

Quite a large number of enthusiasts carry a large, long-handled net that they drop at the water's edge with every move they make along the bank. This tactic is pretty shrewd, because size and weight hold no great disadvantage when the net is out of one's hands, and the angler is literally ready for anything. Certain disadvantages arise when you wander off and leave the thing, only to connect with a rod-bender some quarter mile or so further on. This is Barrie's technique, in fact, and it taught him a lot about landing fish without nets.

Carrying across the back also finds favour, a fair-sized net being mounted on to a handle measured to suit the angler's height, and held with a thong and snap fastening across the shoulders. When one requires the net, a press of the clip at the side lets it drop down into the hand, and the rest is easy. Photo. 6 illustrates this.

Finally, the most universally adopted method is to carry a folding short-handled net slung on a ring at one's waist, ready to be unshipped and flipped out into the extended position for use.

Each style has a little awkwardness about it, which is not helped in any way by the weight factor involved. The drop and carry method produces least worry in this respect — strangely, really large nets made from glass fibre tubes at handle and arms are lighter than any other type. A specimen hunter's net with a 30-inch or more frame is featherlight; the disadvantages being that it is rather cumbersome, and its corners are forever digging into bankside vegetation. A net slung across the shoulder is a convenient way to balance weight, but there is a certain awkwardness about the style when a bag has to be shoulder carried at the same time.

Weight seems to be at its highest concentration in the waist-slung flip-up type of net. The better quality ones have a brass hinge at the knuckle which weighs a ton, together with a heavy metal handle and arms. We feel very lop-sided when we use one, and find that the whole caboodle usually sags so much that the net trails along the ground, to catch in everything imaginable or, worse still, to be trodden on.

There are some lightweight alloy short-handled nets on the market — but they are not suitable for heavy fish or fishing, and if they are slung from an elastic cord are potentially lethal. If the net does catch on the herbage while you carry on walking, the impact when it breaks free to spring back against your body can be quite surprising. It may amuse the fish, but a stunned angler flat on his face in bankside mud is not a pretty sight.

Really it is all a question of how far you are going to walk, how much you have to carry, and what size of fish you could encounter. We use all three styles at one time or another, probably favouring the walk and drop method the most, reasoning that you can never have a landing net that is too big — only too small. But half-way through a day we often regret our decision to use the particular net that we have with us.

The shape of the net frame is a matter of personal preference. Barrie uses a round ring — he feels more confident that a fish is easier to fit into this than any other shape. Ken prefers a triangular rim. He maintains that this can be pushed well into the water, often helping to push down water-weed and that a fish is guided more easily into the actual net itself from this position. We both like our nets to be deep — really deep — so that once the fish is well and truly in the bag it cannot leap out, and we check the mesh at regular intervals for wear or possible tearing. It is possible to buy a triangular frame which packs away, by pulling the arm spreader *down* the handle: the two arms follow it and end up being parallel and close to the handle, and the netting is simply wrapped around both handle and arms. To assemble the net the process is reversed. Obviously, for long hauls along the river bank this type of net is easily packed away.

Micromesh, the new net material, is grand for fish protection, reducing pulling and rasping on their scales. But it is very lightweight, and we have seen problems where the net, once into running water, has turned inside out. The answer to this of course is to stitch a leger bullet into the bottom of the net so that it sinks immediately.

An enormous number of landing nets are ruined every year because anglers will insist on lifting big fish out of the water by holding the end of the handle alone. Do this, and immediately an enormous strain is put on the rim at its joint with the handle. The primary job of a handle is to get the net into a position where a fish can enter it. Once netted, slide your hands down the handle and lift, holding each side of the rim itself. It makes sense — especially at today's replacement prices.

GAFFS AND EMERGENCY ACTION

A large bunch of spinning men carry a gaff slung purposefully at their waist. Ask them why they carry it, and with a slightly incredulous voice, inferring that you must be out of your tiny mind even to ask, they inform you that it is the best and surest tool for landing a fish. We just do not believe them. Further, we tend to think that in a lot of cases the angler is merely adopting a status symbol, something with which to lift himself above the common herd of fishermen.

Now, don't get us wrong. The gaff is a very useful thing, and in the right hands a sure-fire way of getting a fish on to the bank. But it is far from necessary in the vast majority of cases. Once used, it inevitably causes some damage to a fish, even if it is only the risk of disease at the point-wound when it is returned. Worse than this, if the fish has been badly gaffed, gill and stomach wounds can be inflicted that will cause long suffering and unnecessary death.

So our gaffs only receive an outing when we salmon fish or spin a water where we know there might be record-breaking pike. Size is our justification, plus the hope that our catch may grace either a glass case or dinner plate. In fact, of course, the largest landing nets will cope with any pike that swims.

There are an awful lot of gaffs on the market that could never withstand the strain of landing a really good fish. Most faults lie with the collapsible telescopic types made from alloy that, over the seasons, become stiffer and harder to open. Even when opened out, they are also incapable of manhandling 25 lbs or more of struggling fish out of the water and up a bank.

If you need a gaff, then take it from us that they don't come cheap! Steel and brass are expensive and good workmanship, the sort that makes sliding joints silk-smooth to use, add to the bill. We insist that our gaffs have a wide gape, in fact Barrie would like to see a V-shaped hook rather than the usual U-shape that can be difficult to ease into position. U-shaped bends are for salmon fishing, where the gape is needed to assist driving the gaff point into the flanks of the fish.

The point of the jaw is our point of aim when gaffing pike. We are reasonably sure that this portion of the fish will be still — it is held by the hook and line. Once the point is in we lift with the handle held *vertically*, and not at an angle that throws a tremendous strain on the shaft — enough, as we have witnessed in the past, to buckle good metal completely. The only exception to this is on a nice shelving bank when the fish can be slid on to the bank quite easily.

A vertical lift can be quite difficult with wet or cold hands, and there is much to be gained by whipping a leather thong around the gaff handle. One turn round the wrist and hand makes any slipping impossible.

Fixed gaffs, with the steel whipped on to a long rigid handle, are cumbersome to carry but more reliable than the collapsible sort. They also can be shoulder slung, as we described in the landing nets section. But whichever type of gaff you do decide on, for goodness' sake watch that the point is always adequately covered. Most proprietary makes have a fitted point protector — but that didn't stop Ken's daughter shutting her hand between point and protection pad on one occasion. If the protection is a cork, then check at regular intervals that it is still in place. Better still, use a landing net.

Sometimes emergency action is called for. We have all done it at some time: left the net in the car; left it 100 yards down the bank because we forgetfully wandered on; lost it off the waist clip and didn't notice it was missing — or at the best, hooked a fish so big that the net was wholly inadequate. What can be done? Nothing, absolutely nothing, until the fish is completely played out, and absolutely flat on the surface. Then one has the choice of beaching it, or attempting to hand land it by some means or other. Beaching is probably the safest way. Choose the most level piece of bank that you can, tow the fish hard up on to the side, and then drop the rod and grab. Providing that the hooks have not pulled free when the solid resistance of the ground takes over from the glide over the water, you stand a sporting chance. Really it is a matter of speed — and presence of mind in remembering to get the fish right up the bank without bothering to admire it where it lies.

With no level stretch of bank one is rather in the proverbial. There is a choice of attempting to grasp the tail around the wrist, and if you are wearing gloves, then success is reasonably sure. If not, grip like the devil, and hope that the prize doesn't literally slip from your grasp. Gripping the fish at the eyes between finger and thumb and then lifting we regard as a typical piece of Victorian cruelty. Nor are we greatly in favour of sliding our fingers under the gill cover. Quite apart from slight risk of damage to the fish, the hand is too near the hooks for our liking. Pike under 8-9 lbs can be grasped at the back of the head, but it takes a strong man to lift out anything over this weight.

4

Other equipment

THE TAILER

This steel noose, rather like a rabbit snare, is mounted on a handle so that it can be slid over the tail of a fish, and whipped tight over the wrist (just above the tail fin) until it bites, allowing a fish to be lifted out of the water.

Generally used in salmon fishing it is pretty effective, but possessed with one annoying disadvantage in that the steel loop must rest in a a notch to keep it open. We find that it collapses at the slightest knock and half one's day seems to be spent in opening and re-setting it. We have heard of experts who carry the tailer collapsed, and whilst playing a fish can open and prepare it for use — but we are not among that multi-handed few.

SWIVELS

Pick up an antique pike fishing book, glance through the section on spinning, and make mental note of the numbers of swivels that attach to the business end of a line. Usually there was one to the lure, one either end of the trace, and two in the middle of it; a grand total of five. Why? Because swivels were, in those *early* days of mass production, so temperamental that safety was sought in numbers.

With today's products one, or at the most two swivels should be sufficient, although there are some grotty efforts on the market and it does literally pay to be choosy. Consider the straightforward barrel

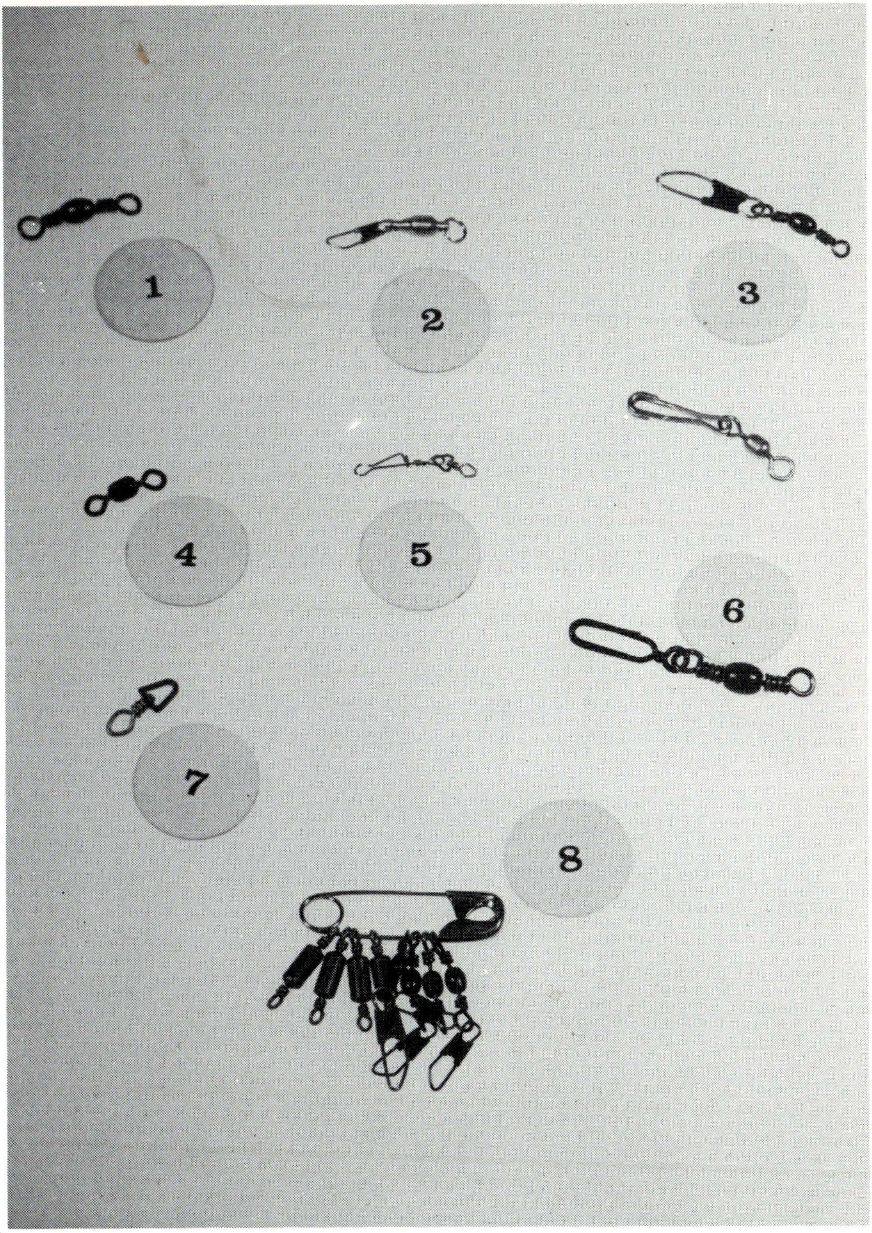

7 SWIVELS. 1. Barrel. 2. American Link. 3. Safety-pin. 4. Berkeley. 5. Diamond Link. 6. Split-link swivels. 7. Diamond. 8. A safe way of carrying. Mixed ball-bearing and safety-pin swivels.

swivel. It looks efficient, turns comfortably in your hand when first it is mounted, but after an outing or two it is an even bet that weed, grit and water will have forced themselves under the casing leaving it with about a 50 per cent efficiency. Moral? Check and lubricate all swivels after a day's fishing. When did you last check yours? Ah!

Next up the scale — and a long way at that financially — is the ball-bearing swivel. This is the Rolls Royce that purrs on forever, needing only an occasional service. Trouble is that it is very difficult to manufacture a small ball-bearing swivel, and those on the market are too big for some of our work.

We have plumped for the diamond swivel for our lighter spinning. The join is a rivet head type that can be seen, and should anything in the way of debris catch round it, can be cleared within seconds. Half a dozen loose swivels in a tackle box can be as elusive as an eel when you want to get hold of one. We clip ours together on a safety pin, which also serves as a good drying rack when we have run a little 3 in 1 oil over them. It's amazing how often you need a safety pin too! The strain of lifting our huge catches can play havoc with buttons.

Link swivels are very much a necessary evil. The idea behind the design is that you should be able to change lures in seconds just by opening the link itself. The problem is that in some cases they either open of their own free will, or worse, pull apart if a sudden strain is thrust through them. The biggest offender in the first case is the spring link swivel. It is opened (with great detriment to one's thumbnail) and the lure slid round into the bight. One, or perhaps one hundred casts later weed forces the springs open, the lure works round through the jaws and drops off.

Some safety pin swivels fall into our second category, with the standing part of the clasp into which the pin shuts suddenly buckling, shedding the lure during retrieval. You pays your money . . . .

We graduated towards the safety pin type, checking that the pin fits well back into the clasp, and that this in turn has a good fold-over. There is an excellent small American ball-bearing link swivel on the market, unfortunately marred because its trace end has a small split ring. These abominations open at the slightest whim, but removed from the swivel they leave a very useful article. There is also a very small diamond link swivel that has a snap-over wire clasp. Great for very fine work, providing one checks regularly for caught-up debris.

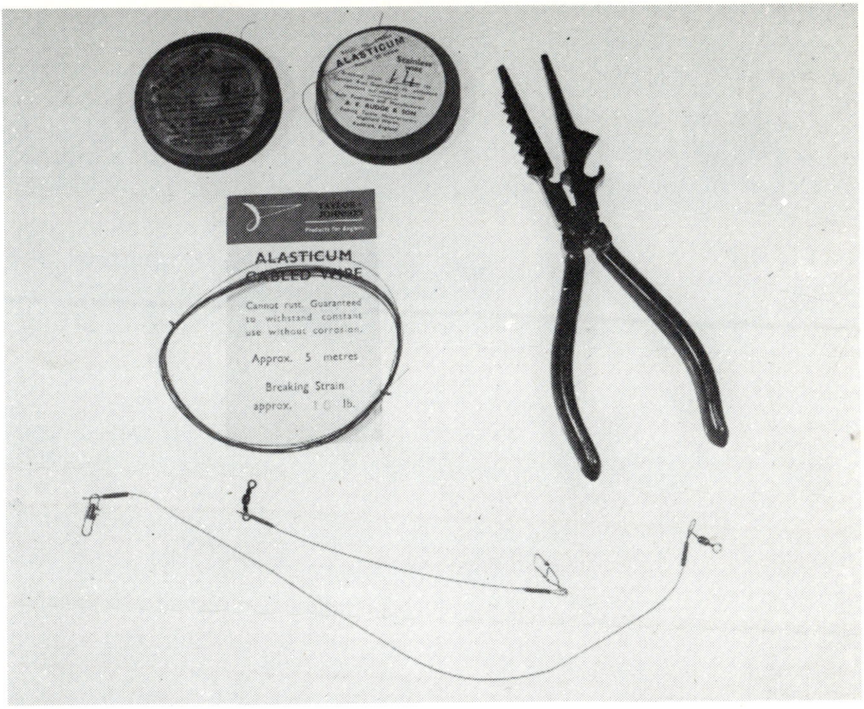

8 Trace-making equipment — with two proprietary traces.

TRACES

If you can avoid using a trace then our advice is to do so. They merely provide another assortment of joins and swivels with possible weakness and wear. But if you do have to use one (and where pike or zander are expected only a fool wouldn't), make sure they are as strong as the line you are using and not a step-down in breaking strain. The popular belief that a trace should have a lower breaking strain than the line probably dates from the good old days of silk, which was a relatively expensive line. A break near the lure left the line intact and the angler little worse off in pocket.

Manufactured traces, usually six to nine inches long, are assembled from nylon coated trace wire with a swivel at one end, and a link swivel at the other. They tend to come in heavy sizes and are rather stiff, and we find that the coating flakes and chips after a time. Glint in strong sun and low water conditions is also quite pronounced.

We make any traces that we require from Alasticum or, better still, Tidemaster or Pegley Davies, matching its breaking strain as near as possible with the actual line strength we are using. Single strand Alasticum is prone to kinking that inevitably precedes a sudden break. We use a 12-15 inch length of cabled wire, which by the time two swivels have been added will make into an approximate 9-12 inch trace. We became dissatisfied with proprietary cabled Alasticum some time ago, and prefer now to twist our own in various breaking strains, a five-minute job using a spun weight or carpenter's hand drill. We also like and use Efgeeco Tidemaster, a stainless steel sorrel-coloured wire twisted with seven strands that, although stiffer than Alasticum, is still soft enough to be made up with one's fingers. Unfortunately it is only available in heavy breaking strains.

Once through the swivel, the cable ends are twisted back on the main strand for about half an inch or so, the surplus snipped off with a good pair of pliers or sharp pair of scissors, and a little Araldite glue spread along the twists to hold the joint firmly in place. Simple, cheap, and the labour of an evening's work can keep one going for a whole season.

ANTI-KINKS AND LEADS

On the majority of days that you spin, line kink will be eliminated by the swivels mounted on the trace or line. But when there is heavy water — a fast current — then the speed at which the lure will turn can present some kinky problems. That is when an anti-kink device of some sort becomes a necessity.

Celluloid anti-kink vanes either clip on to the line with a series of slots, or have a length of looped wire running through them to which the line and trace are attached. The clip-on type will often allow a fine line to turn within the slots, but cope reasonably well with thicker monofilament. Those that are made with a line attachment are better, but again provide yet another joining link between the angler and his fish. We like to keep the number of links on the line to a minimum.

One of our favourite anti-kinks was a vaned torpedo-shaped device called a Kneverkink that slid up the line, and then fastened down on to

9 ANTI-KINKS AND LEADS. 1. Wye lead. 2. Jardine spiral. 3. Celluloid vane. 4. Kneverlink. 5. Hardy Anti-kink. 6. Half-moon leads. 7. Hillman lead. 8. Swan shot.

one half of the swivel from where it could not move. Unfortunately it appears to be out of production now.

But Hardy's have filled the bill with their anti-kink vane that clips on to their ball-bearing swivel. Very efficient in clear water, but weed can dislodge the vane from the swivel body. Note well, and check regularly. The alternative to celluloid or plastic anti-kink vanes is lead in some form or other. Properly applied it will make the swivels work, and as weight will probably be required to keep the lure well down, two purposes can be served with the one application.

The Jardine spiral lead is probably the most popular for spinning. Quite frankly we cannot get on with it. They tend to unravel, and the pulling of line through the bent spiral itself tends to stretch, kink and weaken it. A little better proposition is the Wye lead, its boat shape hanging in such a way that swivels are compelled to move. But they need attaching by either end, and our earlier comment on too many links applies equally here.

Hillman anti-kink leads that clip on to one eye of a swivel are excellent, except when they catch on the bottom or in weed beds, something they tend to do with monotonous regularity. Which leaves us with large split shot or fold-over half moon leads, and these are our favourites. But we are cautious enough to test both types of lead when we buy them, making sure that they really are soft. It is so very easy to pinch the line with hard shot, causing a weakness that is concealed and irreparable damage.

BOXES

People spin because they like to be mobile, choosing to search for their fish, which is a very sound argument for keeping unnecessary tackle to a minimum. Apart from one or two boxes containing changes and spare baits, a few traces and some odd swivels and trebles, the only other items we pack are a small pocket torch for early morning and late evening work, a set of scales or a measure of some sort for recording in our notebooks the details of fish we catch — a source of information for future outings — and some means of removing hooks from the fishes' mouths.

Fortunately, fish taken spinning are almost invariably hooked in the mouth, and deep surgery is unnecessary. But the sheer force exerted by a fish seizing a spinner often drives the hooks hard into the bony structure of the jaw itself. Forceps are an obvious necessity under these circumstances, or better still a pair of pliers (Abu produce a first-rate pair) that not only serve for hook removal, but also help in any first aid to metal work that may be needed on trace or lure.

Compared to the coarse and plug fisherman the spinning enthusiast's problem of carrying his lures around is relatively easy. No tremendous bulk, no chunky thicknesses or diving vanes with odd angles; on the contrary, the majority of spinning lures are fairly flat, and although perhaps rather heavy, only present a problem where hooks and swivels can tangle. Of course, few anglers are solely one kind of fisherman or the other.

We select boxes that are slim and small so that they fit easily into a pocket. There are umpteen proprietary makes on the market that are

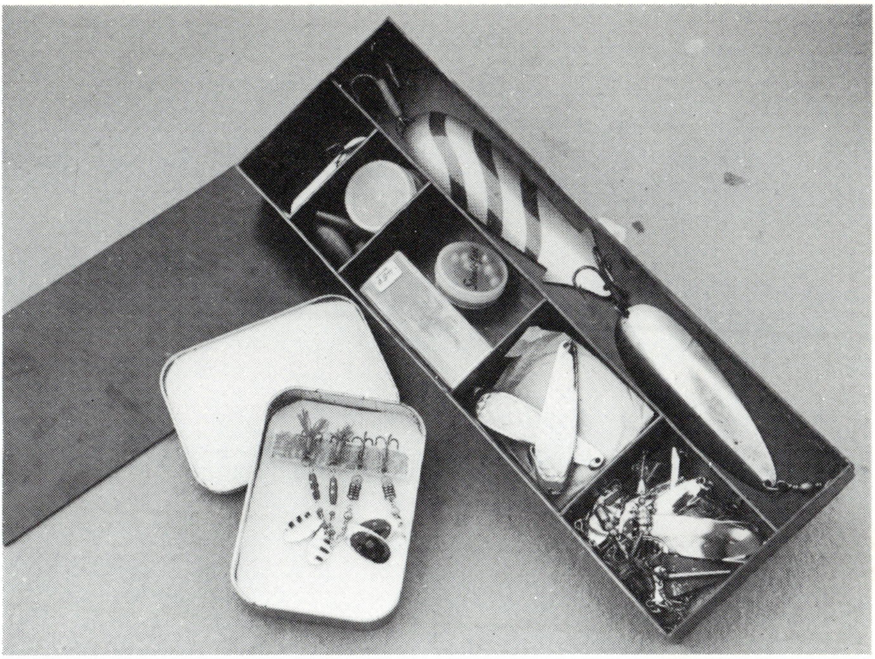

10 Barrie's home-made tackle box, and one of Ken's conversions out of a tobacco tin.

admirable, but we prefer those that have a transparent lid — not so much that we can see what we want, but because the effect of opening a box held upside down produces a fall-out too horrific for words. Most purchased boxes are ready divided, and the majority of lures can be fitted in one way or another. But, of course, this way of packaging does lead to a certain amount of tangle.

The only way of curing this time-waster is to glue strips of balsa wood or cork into small tin boxes, and firmly hook each treble into them. By further adding foam to the bottom of the box it is also possible to kill an enormous amount of metallic jangle that sounds great at the beginning of the day, but soul-destroying at its end. One of the best materials for this is Etherfoam, obtainable in bulk from Dons of Edmonton.

Barrie has tried making his own boxes following advice from Dave Holden (see also his article in the magazine *Coarse Fisherman* for Dec. 1976). All you need is Slater's plasticard in various thicknesses and colours, a glue such as Weldite, a Stanley knife, and a ruler. You can make strong boxes of almost any shape or size with very little practice: the one illustrated (Photo. 10) took a little over half an hour to make.

One thing is certain, that after a few years' spinning you will, like the fly fisherman, collect an awful amount of surplus baits of various sorts, sizes and condition. Hardy favourites wax and wane, and a new spinner becomes top of the pops; but, of course, one never thinks of ditching

11 Proprietary pocket boxes and the home reservoir for keeping spinners.

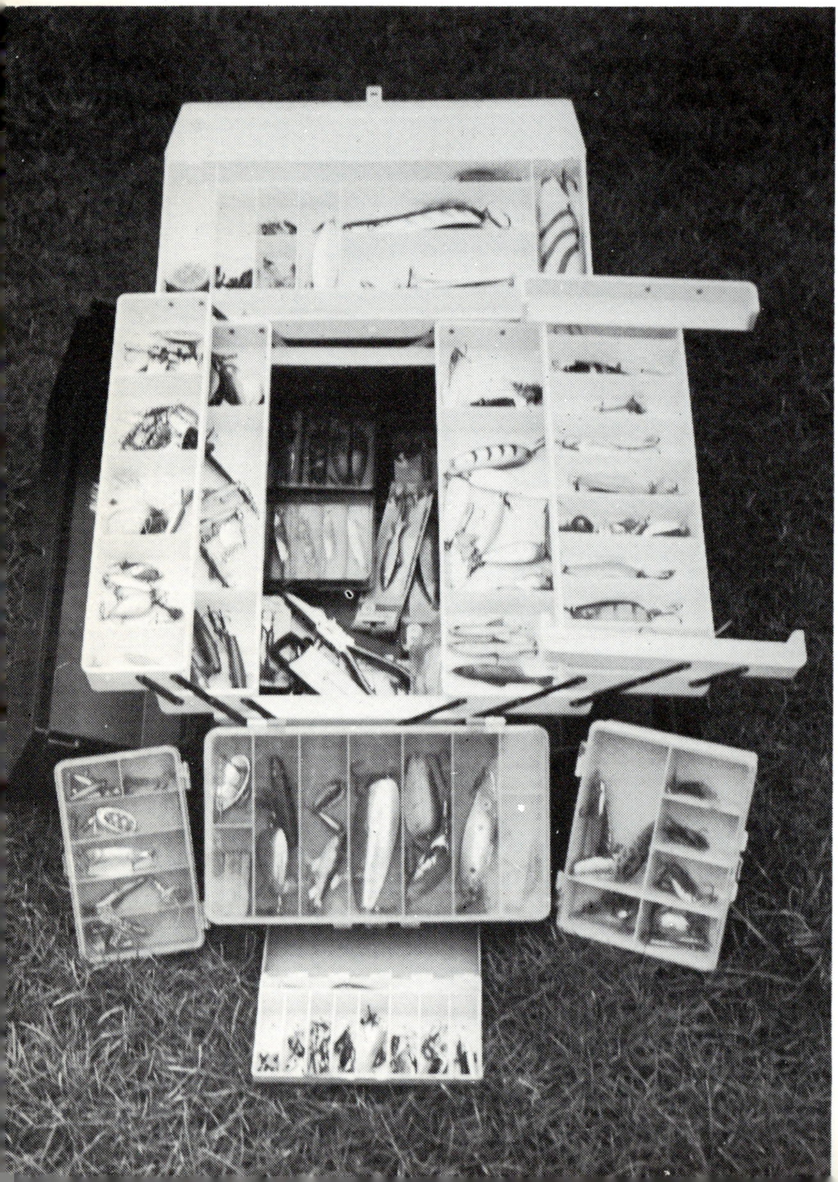

that which is out-dated. The only sensible way of keeping a check on things and preventing good material from rusting and rotting is to use a base camp, a large lure box into which the excesses and reserves can be kept. Ken illustrates his in Photo. 11. Despite the amount of room it occupies in his den, it remains a thing of beauty, and a source of pleasurable winter rummaging.

CLOTHING

What you wear when you fish is a matter of personal preference and very often price. In fact, apart from waterproof clothing few anglers bother to tog-up for the sport, using every-day coats and trousers that, judging by appearance, are nearing the evenings of their sartorial lives.

We certainly are not bankside spivs, but we do observe several essential points when we robe for the sport. As an example, in summer we never confuse light clothing with bright, knowing full well that it is impossible to keep below the sky line all of the time and that fish can see. We also make sure that any shirt we wear has long sleeves, having suffered the pains of sunburn in our youth, and follow the old countryman's dodge of taking more clothing with us than we may reasonably need. Too often in the past we have spent the day frozen to the marrow when forecasted sun has failed to appear.

Footwear can be a summer problem. The temptation to wade is often at its greatest, not necessarily to cast to a fish, but perhaps to reach a particular place that is unapproachable when the water is high. If one decides on knee or thigh waders despite the heat, take an extra pair of socks and change them during the day. Feet soaking with perspiration have a curious psychological effect, and make you feel ten times hotter than you really are.

Although the current trend seems to be towards one-piece suits for winter wear we have avoided them. They may be exceptionally warm, but we find that the one-piece construction restricts movement to the point where it becomes tiring. Also their lack of pockets means that various small items of equipment have to be carried separately in a bag — again, a restriction to movement.

Loose-fitting woollies, a jacket with loads of pockets, and waders, with a good waterproof outer jacket of some sort take a lot of beating, with perhaps a woollen bobble hat to cover the ears. Hats as such we find a nuisance during windy weather and of little protection when it rains. To look left or right when wearing a hood usually means turning one's whole body, because the hood is attached at the shoulders and does not move with your head.

One item of clothing that we have gone out of our way to invest in has been the fly fisherman's waistcoat. Ideal for summer wear, and just as useful under a waterproof in winter, the vast array of pockets with their self-sealing flaps can carry a multitude of spinners and odds and ends, as our picture shows.

12 The fly-fisherman's waistcoat — equally useful for the spinning man.

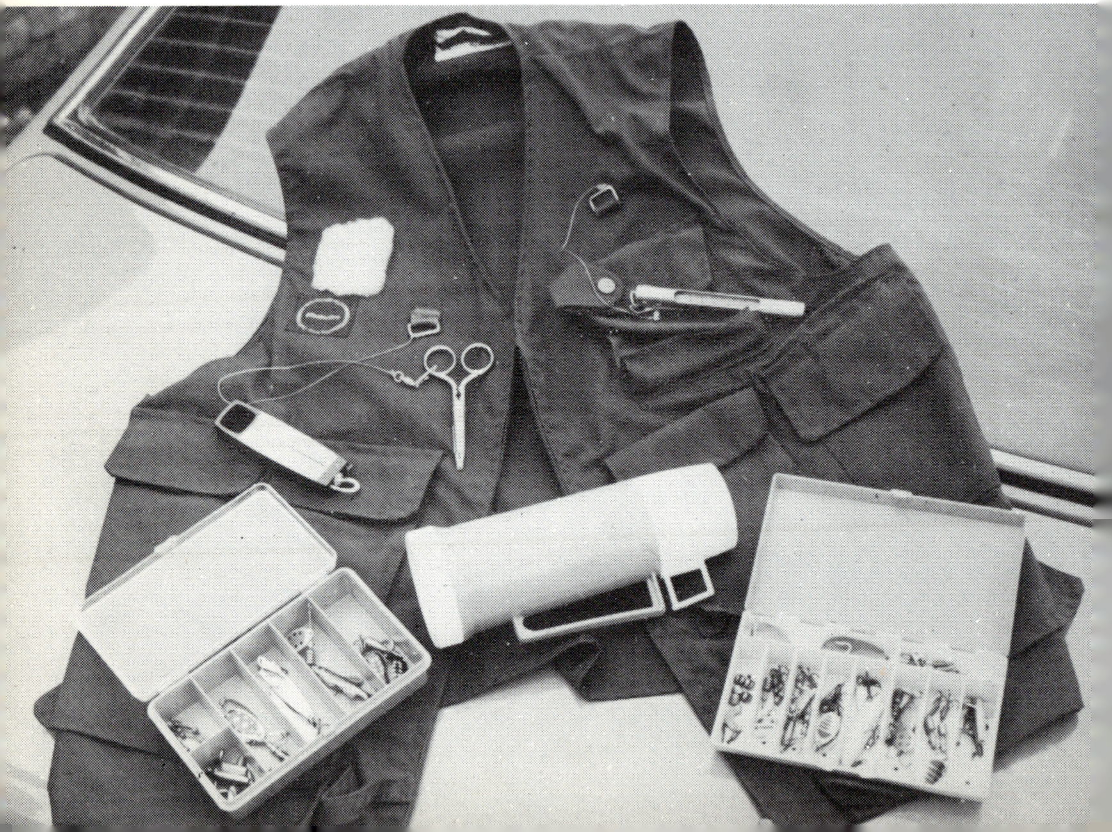

PART TWO

Spinners, spoons and baits

5

Definitions and variety

At a first consideration you might think a definition of spoon or spinner unnecessary, but anglers are notoriously casual people, we're happy to report, and use words and phrases which will give no clue to the beginner of their real intentions or activities. For example, we often say 'We're just going off to do a bit of spinning' when what we really mean is that we're going to hump a huge box of lures consisting of spinners, spoons, plugs (and a few others besides): we're not merely going to use spinners. Then there's that word 'lure'. Not so many years ago its usage was largely confined to plugs, spoons and spinners, the rest being baits and flies, but today it applies also to a special form of large fly (which some people would scathingly refer to as a spinner or plug!) used by reservoir trout anglers. So it is important, at least to us, to define what we mean by spinners, spoons, and wobbled baits.

Almost certainly we cannot do this without upsetting somebody. When we wrote *Plugs and plug fishing* we included a definition of what we considered a plug to be. No less an authority than Brian Harris, the editor of the monthly glossy magazine *Angling*, disagreed with our definition and defined a plug as 'a lure that attracts predatory fish at the surface and below it by wobbling or wriggling but not spinning'. In our opinion this definition of a plug also applies to big spoons that are bounced through big waves or across the choppy surfaces of lakes, techniques which, as we shall describe, have been shown in recent years to be highly successful fish-catching methods.

Our definition of a spinner would, therefore, be:
an artificial bait, usually made of metal (but also of plastic, wood, quill and rubber), often in the shape of a blade (but also as a tube) rotating or spinning

about a bar or axis, to which it may be attached at one end only, or along the whole of its length.

And our definition of a spoon:
a spoon shaped blade, usually with a treble attached at the tail end and a swivel at the front end; it usually wobbles rather than spins, so that there is no linear axis.

Now all spoons do not wobble, as many anglers mistakenly think. In our experiments in flume tanks we found that some famous spoons, Toby's for example, actually spin strongly under certain current or retrieve conditions, so that some spoons act like and are akin to other kinds of lures, undoubtedly spinners, which never wobble. At the other extreme we have spoons such as the Piker which always wobble under normal fishing conditions. We could refer to these as wobbled baits, but that is a title we prefer to use for natural fish baits that are retrieved with a wobble: *spun* natural baits are treated at length in chapter 8. So to conclude this short account of definitions, we leave you with the above two definitions and a realization that spinners and spoons form a continuous spectrum, the ends of which are linked by spoons that spin.

The main types of spinners (plug-like spinners; bar-spoons; fly-spoons; mackerel spinners; minnows and wagtails) and spoons (Toby's; Copper and Silver; Jim Vincent and Piker) are described and illustrated in chapter 6. Fig. B is a flow diagram relating the various types, including the borderline types which are discussed immediately below.

Spinner/plug gradations
A number of famous spinners have a head, sometimes of rubber, leading the revolving bar-spoon: the Voblex is the most well-known to British anglers; but Bomber's Gimmick (Fig. C) is another good one with a weighted head which also acts as a built-in and highly efficient anti-kink device.

Spinner/fly gradations
Fly-spoons have been well known and effective for trout and perch for many years: almost always they consist of a spoon-like blade which *spins* about an axis of swivels or wire, and a following fly tied on a single hook (sometimes a treble hook, as in Russian fly-spoons). They can be regarded as bar-spoons with fly added, but can be fished very effectively

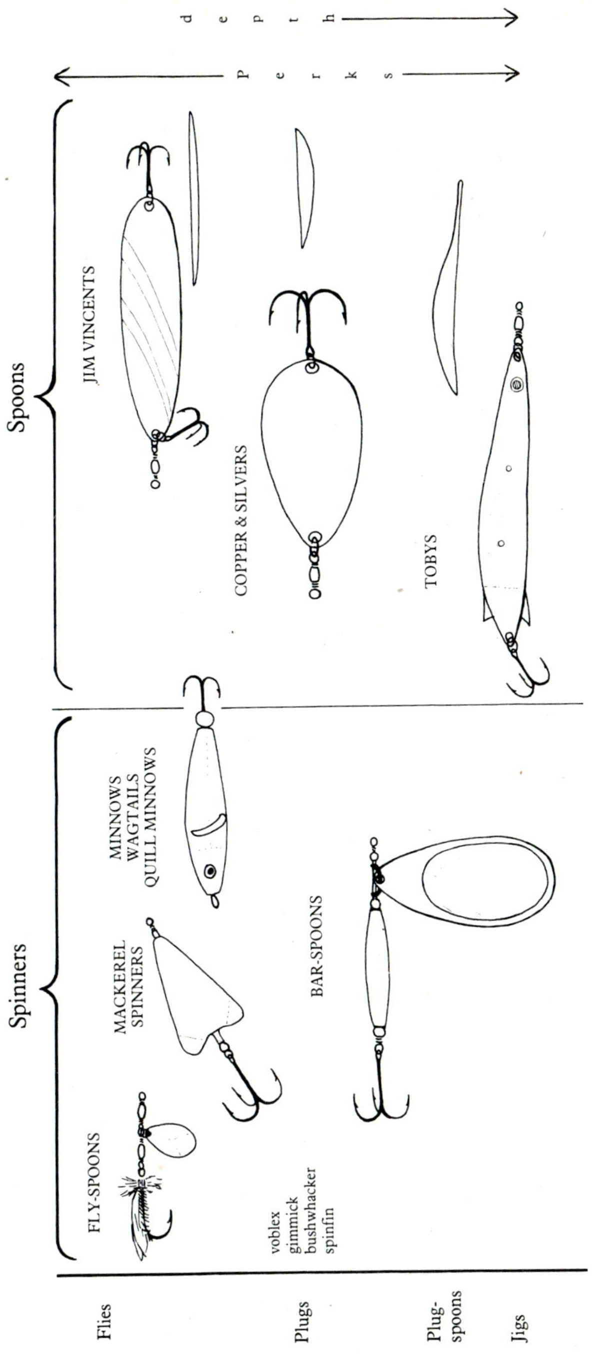
depth
perks
Spoons
JIM VINCENTS
COPPER & SILVERS
TOBYS
Spinners
FLY-SPOONS
MACKEREL SPINNERS
MINNOWS
WAGTAILS
QUILL MINNOWS
BAR-SPOONS
voblex
gimmick
bushwhacker
spinfin
Flies
Plugs
Plug-spoons
Jigs

Fig. **B**

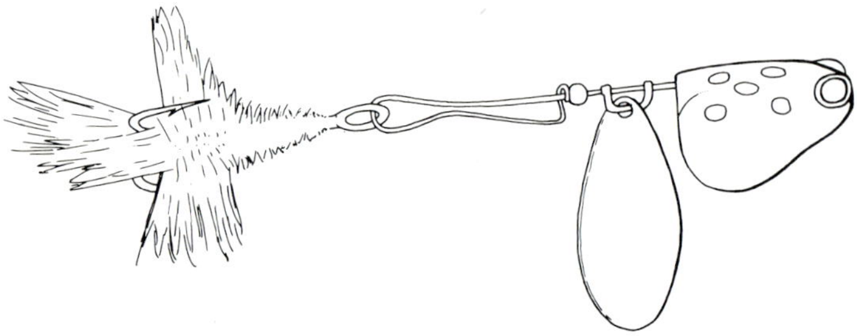

Fig. **C**

without a fly. Indeed some anglers, perhaps rightly, consider a fly-spoon to be a lure that can be cast with a fly rod.

Additives to spinners will be discussed at various sections of the text following.

Spinner/spoon gradations

We have already mentioned that Toby spoons, and others, may *spin*. Some 'weedless' spoons such as the Russian form (Fig. D) either spin, slide or wobble depending upon conditions, and certain anti-kink spoons do as much spinning as wobbling.

Spoon/plug/fly gradations

This is a very important category, because here we would place Bomber's Bushwhacker range (Fig. E) with its one or more largely wobbling, flashing spoons above a crude-looking, large-headed fly of sorts. Its importance is that it is one of the best 'weedless' lures on the market and can be fished through lily pads and other difficult situations with great success: it combines the main attributes of spoon, plug and fly and arranges them in such a fashion that the leading wires tend to part the weed. Very similar, and equally effective, is Heddon's Spin-fin.

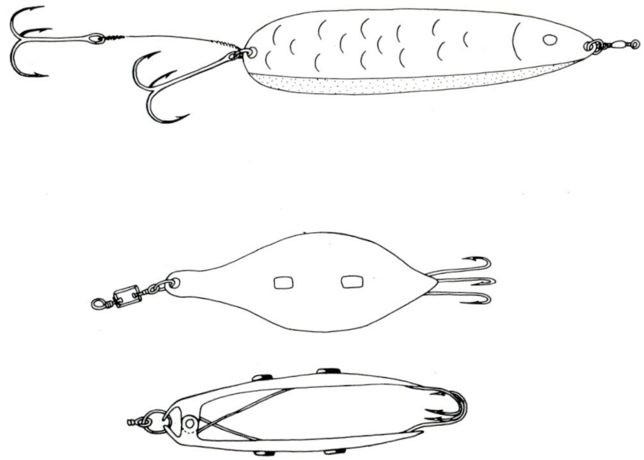

Fig. **D**

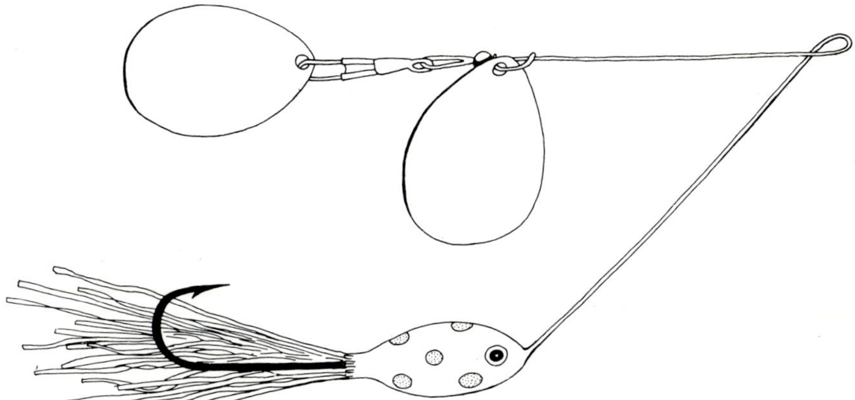

Fig. **E**

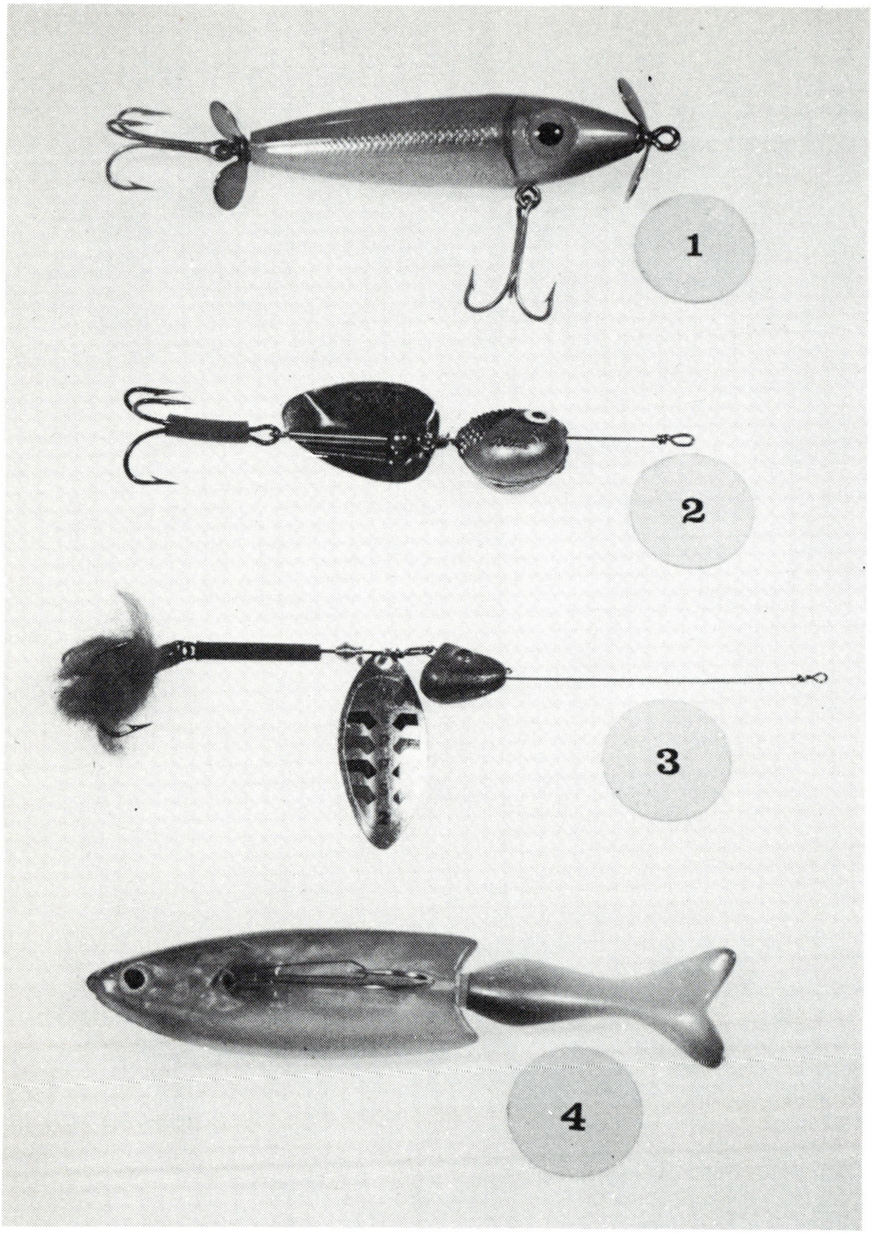

13 PLUG SPINNERS. Sinner Spinner. 2. The Voblex. 3. Mepps Adour. 4. Heddon Commando.

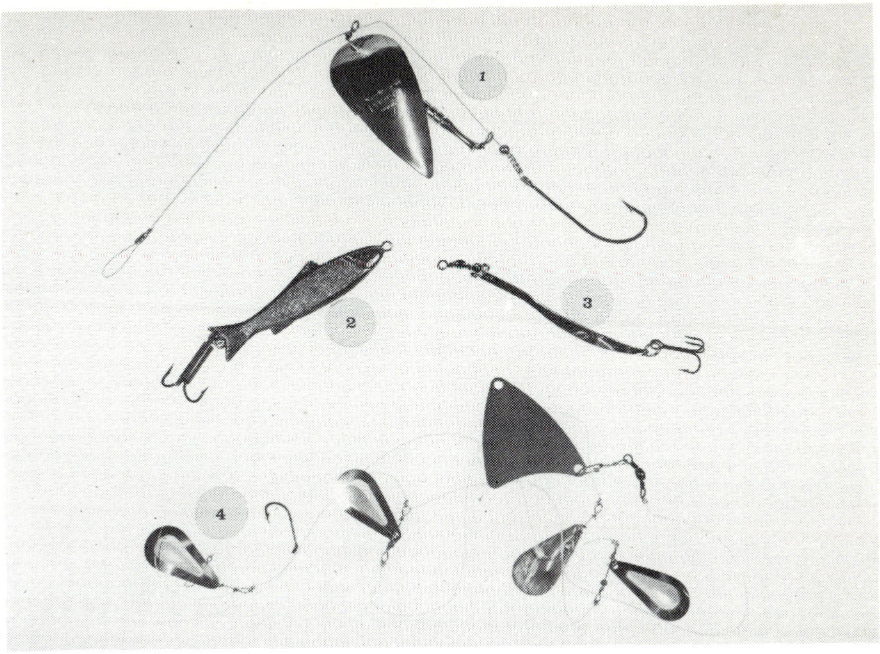

14 PERKS. 1. Normark Vibro. 2. Shakespeare Troller. 3. Shakespeare Condor Bar. 4. Abu Konvoj.

Plug/spoons

There are very few in this category. The plug/spoon we illustrated in *Plugs and plug fishing* is essentially a metal plug and we shall consider it here no further; but Creek Chub's Cohokie is a genuine spoon but highly unusual in that the blade is flat-lying, and wobbles in a spoon-like fashion. There is surely great need for experiment with flat-lying spoons.

Jigs and perks

Jigs are more akin to plugs and many look just like plugs, but are worked essentially vertically below a boat or bridge, or on short casts between weed beds and undercut banks (Fig. F). Perks are fished in similar fashion, but they look more like a very heavy spoon. Indeed, spoons can be used as perks under certain circumstances. Both jigs and perks require the acquisition of a great deal of skill on the part of the user: it is not simply a question of chucking them out and jerking them in again.

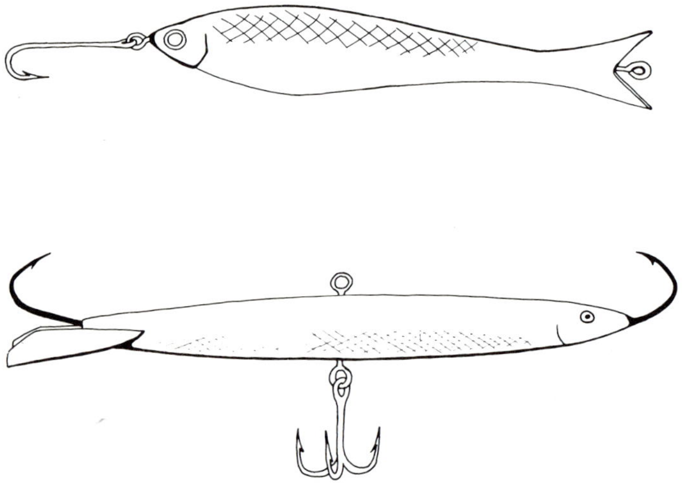

Fig. **F**

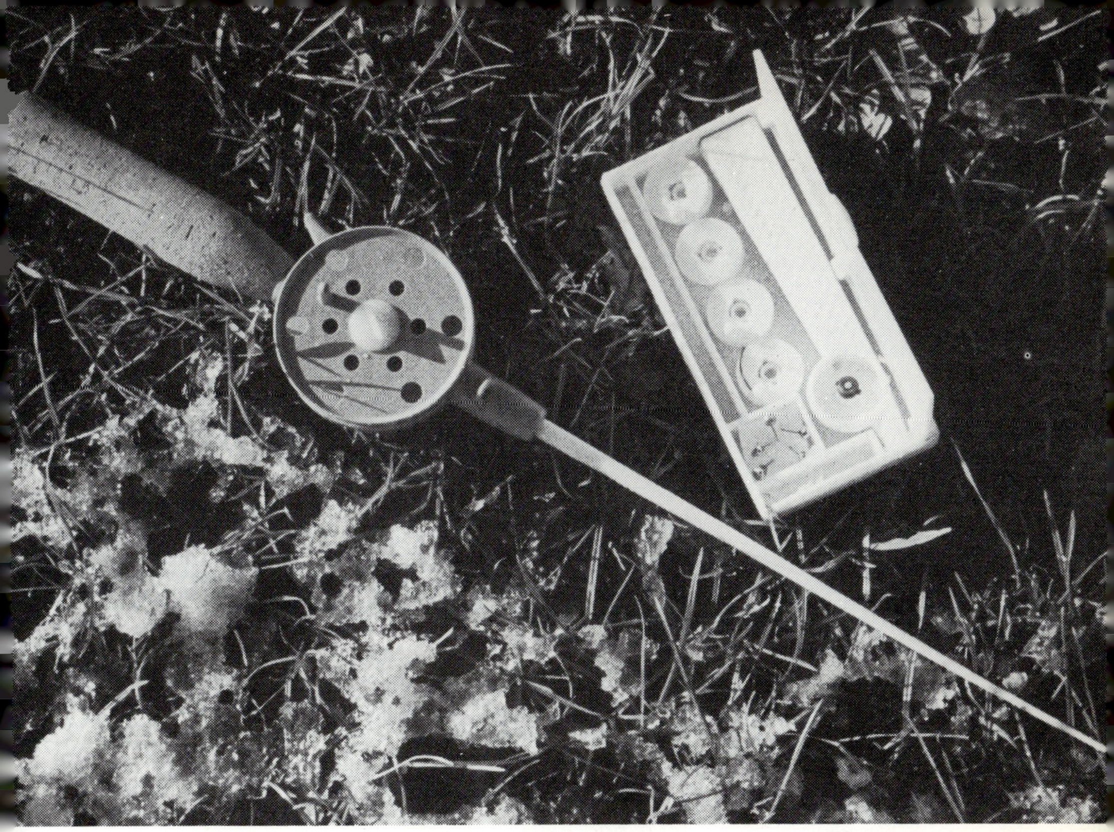

15 Ice fishing jigs from Russia.

6

Spinners and spoons: basic types

In the previous chapter on definitions and variety it can be seen that in Fig. B (page 45) we have placed *Bar-spoons* in a very central position parallel with what we call the *Copper and Silvers*. Bar-spoon is obviously a slight misnomer, very entrenched in angling literature, for bar-spoons are spinners and can be contrasted with the C & S *spoons* which largely wobble. The two types form the basic core of the spinning man's lure box.

Bar-spoons are deadly, and include many types well known to British anglers, such as Veltic, Ondex, Vibro and Mepps to arrange them in order of increasing weight for any one size of blade. Immediately a retrieve is begun the blades revolve, bite deeply into the water and produce a very strong vibration. The Vibro, made by Normark, causes the top rod of any reasonably light spinning rod to bend and judder, but with all these spinners there is real *feel* on the retrieve. If everything goes slack whilst reeling in, two things can have happened: either the lure has picked up weed, or a fish has taken the lure and continued swimming towards you in a classic slack line bite. Both situations should be treated in the same manner, namely with a sweeping strike. In the case of the weeded lure the strike may dislodge the weed, or else start the blade spinning again in spite of the encumbrance: and fish *will* occasionally take a lure trailing weed from the hooks. If it's a slack line bite then the sweeping strike may connect with the fish.

Making bar-spoons is easy, as can be seen on page 64, but here we want to explain the basically similar nature of the various types. Firstly there is a swivel at the head of the lure. Attached to this is a bar, which gives the name bar-spoon, and this runs along the axis to be attached by various means to a treble hook at the rear of the lure. There are two

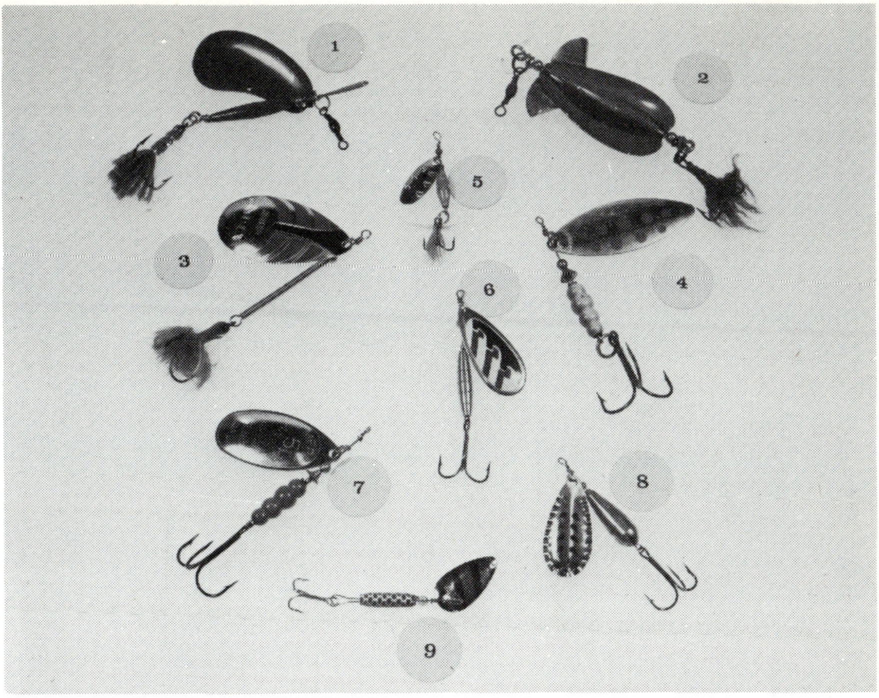

16 BAR-SPOONS. 1. Kidney Spoon. 2. Colorado Spinner. 3. Ondex. 4. Mepps Aglia (leaf). 5. Abu Colibri. 6. T.A.F.F. 7. Mepps Aglia. 8. Abu Droppen. 9. Shakespeare Kilko.

additions to this axial arrangement. One is the crux of the whole lure, namely a spoon-shaped blade attached at one end (Photos. 16 and 24) so that it spins *very freely and loosely* about the axis. The second additive is weight, usually placed behind the blade and in front of the treble hook. Various bar-spoons have plenty of weight here (Mepps, Shakespeare and Intrepid bar-spoons), others have much less (Veltic and Ondex). Light bar-spoons can be fished in very shallow and weedy water, and are essentially short range lures, whereas the heavier ones cast much further and can be fished deep quite easily. All can be retrieved very slowly, and in general the slower the better. Also, as a generalisation, we have found a steady retrieve to be more successful than a variable and jerky one. Both these remarks should be taken only as a rough guide, for trout sometimes need a very quickly drawn spinner;

whilst a bar-spoon fished sink and draw style can be quite killing, that is by raising the rod top thus pulling the vibrating bar-spoon upwards, and then dropping the tip sharply so that the spoon flashes and flutters downwards.

Further additions to the basic bar-spoon pattern take the form of feather or wool to the tail treble, and various colourations or indentations of the blade. The value of these particular additions is discussed in the appropriate places in the text below.

An addition which really adds up to a slightly different kind of lure is achieved by placing a head *in front* of the blade (Fig. C on page 46). In the most well known form, the Voblex, the head is of rubber; in others it may be of heavier material and strongly attached to the bar axis so that it behaves as a built-in anti-kink device. Spinners like the Voblex are really part way to being plugs: they have plenty of weight, cast like bullets, and are really top-class spinners.

Fly-spoons, too, are in the basic bar-spoon pattern (Photo. 17). The axes in these are usually wire or a string of swivels, the blade revolves in the usual way, but is sometimes attached so that it flutters rather than spins, and the treble hook at the rear is almost always replaced by a single hook carrying a fly often of recognised pattern such as a Silver Doctor. Generally speaking, fly-spoons are smaller than the average bar-spoon, and lighter, and are intended for delicate short range fishing with light lines. They are excellent for many species of fish but were intended for trout in low water conditions. We have fished them for small brownies and seatrout on moorland streams with considerable success, and here it must be remembered that each retrieve may be no more than a few yards each cast.

At this point we should contrast the spoon-like blade of these bar-spoons and fly-spoons with the Copper and Silvers. Generally, the blade on a bar-spoon is of shallower curvature than that of wobbling spoons proper, and they are never concavo-convex so far as we know. In the Vibro the unattached end of the blade is pointed, a factor which contributes largely to the tremendous vibration set up by this bar-spoon during the retrieve. Some bigger fly-spoons have quite a convex blade with a three-faceted surface, but these are rather unusual and may well be out of production. In the kidney spoon, a classic bar-spoon with a leaded axis, the blade is kidney-shaped, and the rotation is distinctly slower and more intermittent than in any of the types mentioned above.

All the spinners discussed so far are the basic bar-spoon type, but what is in effect a much more drastic change than any yet considered is to attach the spinning blade along the whole of its length, but in a fashion that still enables it to spin about a straight axis. The result can take two forms: one with a still recognisable blade such as the famous mackerel spinner (Photo. 41(4)) and the second where the 'blade' is roughly shaped like a fish as in wagtails, quill and other minnows (Photo. 18). These are still spinners in the strictest sense with a straight axis through a spinning body. Mackerel spinners borrowed, as the name suggests, from sea-fishing circles, we rate as one of the best and cheapest on the market, particularly for pike in shallow, weedy waters where we have taken literally thousands of fish. They are not that easy to make, but fortunately are very cheap. Quill minnows are easy enough to make, and in trout fishing hill country, such as the Lake District, Wales and Scotland, many village shops sell them made by the local expert. Photo. 18 (6) gives some idea of their hook-bristling appearance. As a rule they are nicely painted, with eyes on, as are the wooden and metal minnows, but all this detail may be wasted on fish, as we suggest in chapter 7. The *general* colour is probably important but not the detail. All these forms of

17 FLY-SPINNERS & SPOONS. 1. The Roachtickle. 2. Mepps Mouche Noire. 3. Fly-spoon — with fly. 4. Abu Fly. 5. Plain Fly-spoon.

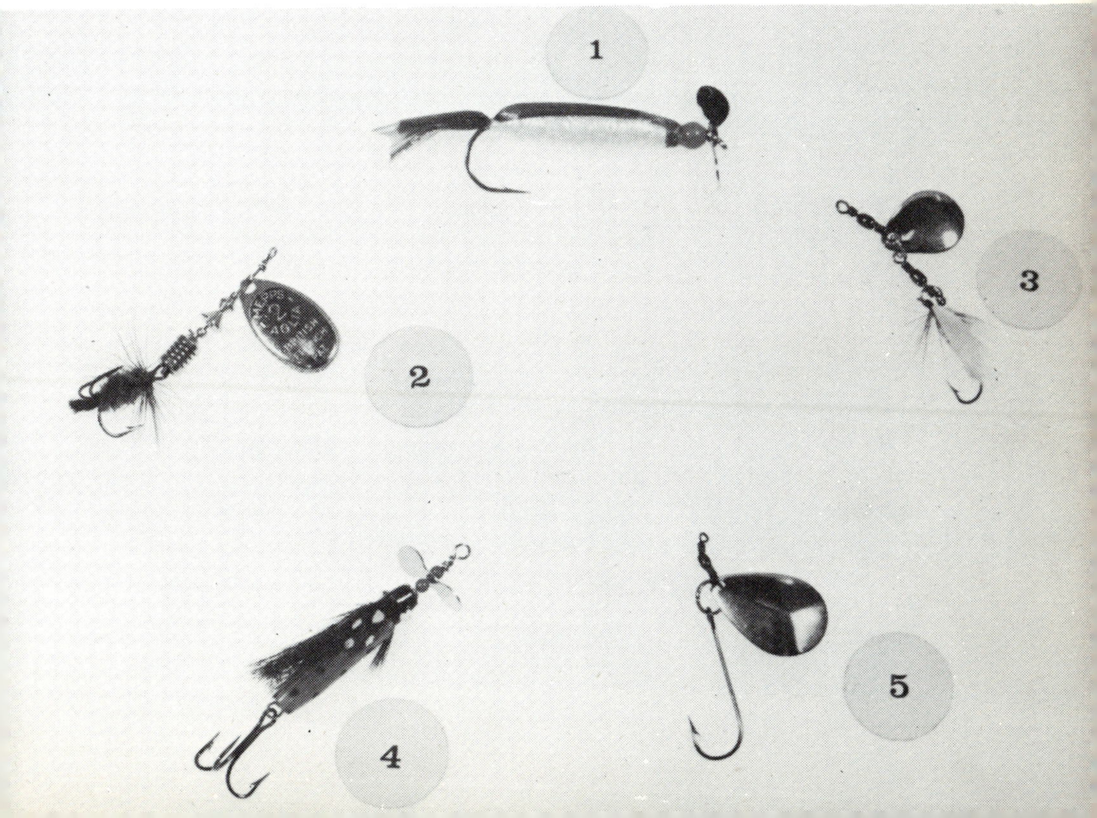

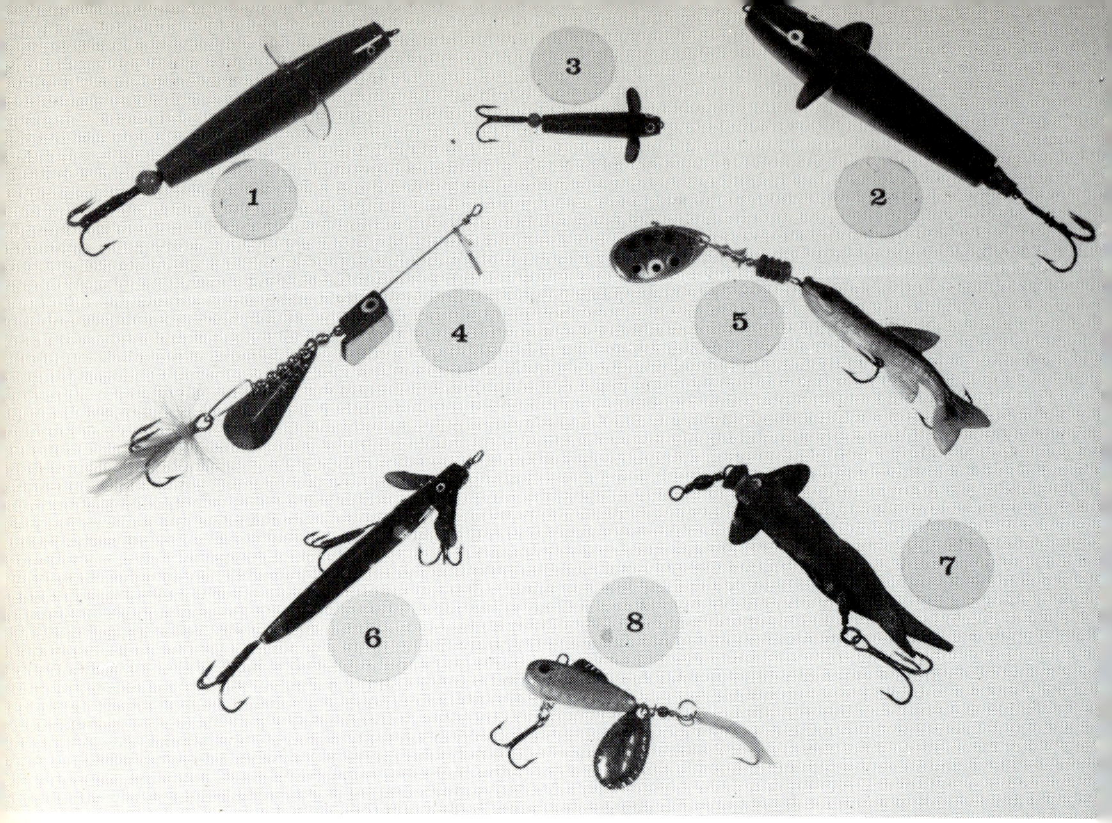

18 1. Wooden Devon. 2. Plastic Devon. 3. Metal Devon. 4. Morrum Spinner (Abu). 5. Mepps Mino. 6. Quill Minnow. 7. Wagtail. 8. Abu Spin-up.

artificial minnows are tried and proven baits for trout and salmon but are very effective indeed for perch, pike and chub.

The Colorado spoon is a famous *spinner*, often denigrated by the modern pike angler, probably unjustly in our experience. The spoon-like blade is attached at both ends to the axial bar (Photo. 16) which is also leaded. But more important are two fins at the front of the spoon: these are set in opposite senses so that the blade as a whole spins strongly. It would be interesting to know the origins of this spinner, relative to the Copper and Silver spoons which we discuss in the following paragraph.

The next main category to think about is the Copper and Silvers (Fig. B). We use this title merely in the sense that it is central to that part of the figure, and that the simple dessert-spoon-shaped lure is one of the oldest in angling history. Perhaps the classic version has about a 3-inch spoon, of relatively heavy metal, and is copper coloured on the inside and silver on the outside — hence the title name we have chosen.

All the spoons in this section do not usually spin about an axis but wobble upon a variously erratic course. The piker (Photo. 19), for example, may deviate from a straight line by as much as 12 inches even on a steady retrieve.

Spoons like the C & S (Photo. 19) with their egg-shaped outline, and dessert-spoon convexity were the first spoons we made ourselves from the family cutlery, and are still the mainstay of Irish pike trollers. Probably most youngsters do this at some time or other, and having conned the old man into drilling a hole at each end, add a split ring and swivel at the narrow end and a split ring and treble hook at the fat end — and there you have a perfectly satisfactory, highly efficient spoon which rarely fails to work. The convexity combined with weight are the two variables which decide whether a spoon of this type will wobble well, and it may be necessary to get to work with a round-headed hammer to effect some changes of shape.

If we take this shape as the basic and classic spoon shape, there are various ways we can effect changes. Simplest, of course, is to change the

19 SPOONS. 1. Piker. 2. Salamander. 3. Abu Toby. 4. Plain Copper Spoon.

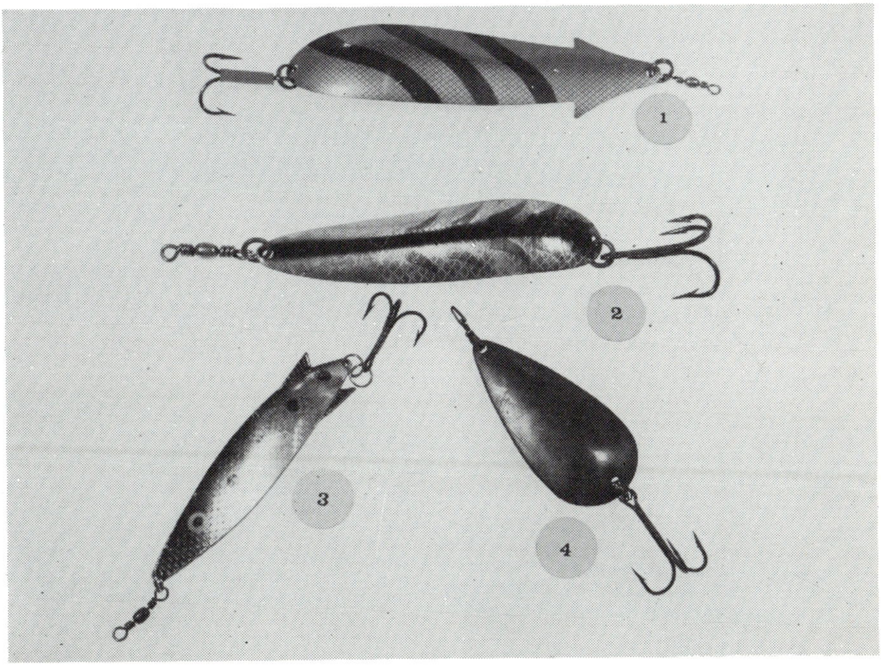

colour. The standard Irish trolling spoon is copper-coloured on the inside and silver on the convex outside, but they can be copper all over, silver all over, red inside, or any combination of stripes and spots that the angler fancies. We shall return to this matter of colour in chapter 7, when dealing with making your own spoons.

More drastic changes are effected by altering the outline of the spoon. For example, instead of being short and egg-shaped it can be elongated (Photo. 20) as in the case of the Jim Vincent spoons. In light metal (or wood, as was the *original* J. V. spoon and similar spoons used by the Red Indians) these are superb for fishing shallow broads and meres, particularly when trolled or trailed behind a boat. In heavier metal they can be cast better, avoiding the planing so common with light spoons, and can be fished more easily in deep water. The basic Jim Vincent style spoons, that is elongate, convex on one side and correspondingly concave on the other, and coming in all sorts of different brands, colours, sizes and weights, are just about the most effective of all

20 SPOONS. 1. Shakespeare De Luxe. 2. Abu Atom. 3. Abu Mortblank. 4. Shakespeare Jim Vincent. 5. Plain Silver Spoon. 6. Norwegian Paravan. 7. Shakespeare Catcher.

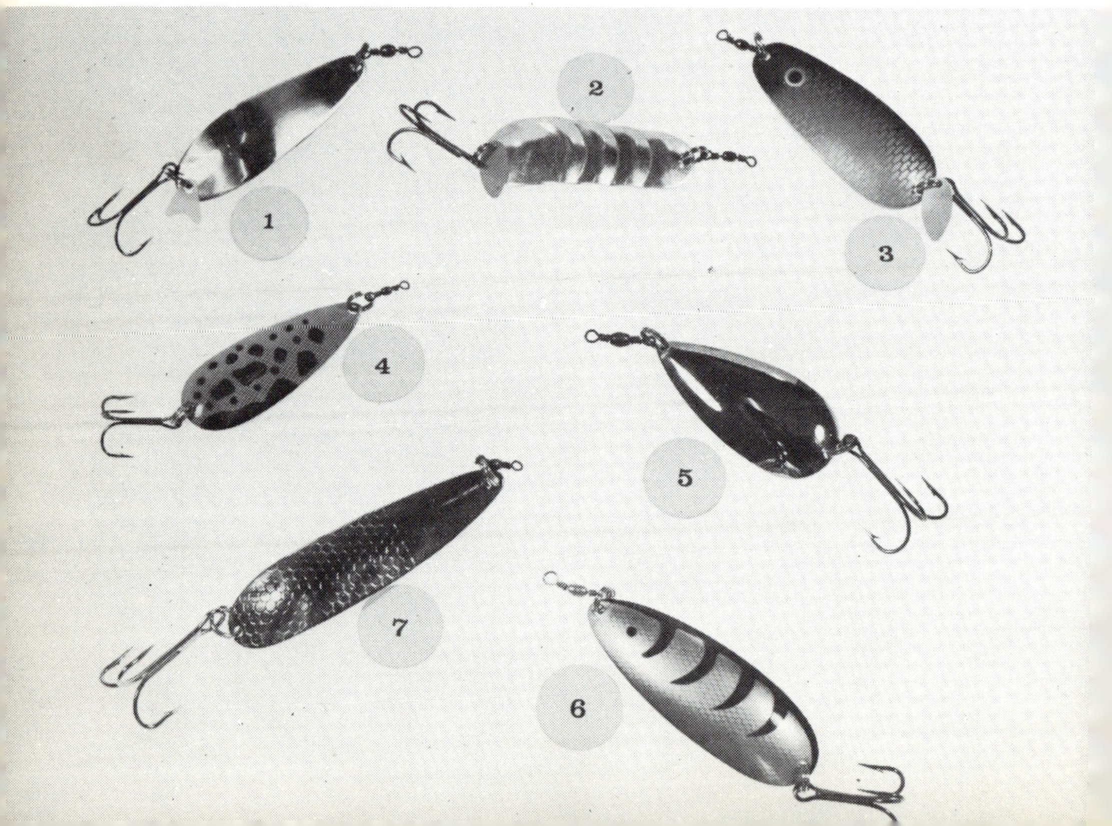

artificial lures. It is possible to have a weight, size or colour for almost all situations.

The next change to consider is that of altering the actual spoon shape itself by making it concavo-convex, usually convex on the outside towards the rear of the spoon. In the Gresvig Crocodile made by Paravan of Norway the spoon is still essentially convex on the outside, whereas in Gladding's Intrepid Flasha range the spoon is *flat* but S-shaped or sigmoidal when viewed from its edge. The latter range has flectolite added to the outside to give numerous reflecting surfaces. Toby spoons are about half-way between Flashas and Crocodiles in their overall convexity, are similarly concavo-convex along their length, but have in addition two tiny stabilizer-like fins near the rear of the spoon, which are directed slightly outwards rather than inwards (Photo. 19(3)). Each of these spoons has a slightly differing action, they are heavier than the basic C & S and Jim Vincent patterns, and cast rather better. Under certain conditions they have a tendency to *spin* about a slightly wobbly axis.

Finally we would mention the Piker spoon, a lure designed for the modern pike angler, combining the elongate spoon-shape of the Jim Vincent, the concavo-convex outline in edge-on view, and a thin metal construction enabling it to be fished in shallow water, and retrieved at the surface by bouncing it through big waves. Like the Toby it has a couple of 'stabilizers' but these are at the front of the spoon, not the back. Barrie used to use a similarly concavo-convex spoon some 6 inches long for trolling the Irish Loughs, but found its fish catching improved dramatically after it had been roughly converted from a Toby shape to a Jim Vincent shape.

Probably anyone reading this part of our book will be itching to say that all this is very well but spoons are very easy to make in all different shapes and sizes. This is true, and we hope we've catered for this instinct in chapter 7, but the home handyman will find that most of his efforts classify quite naturally into the basic types we have just described, and which commercial lure makers have been producing for many years. You can add all sorts of things, extra trebles, trailing trebles (Commando spoons), plastic tags, garish colours, fur and feather, and the bulk still fall into the Toby, C & S, and Jim Vincent patterns.

7

Spinner making and spinner action

Spoons are rather easier to make than bar-spoons, mackerel spinners or minnows, so we shall begin with and concentrate upon them. It should be said at the outset that neither of us are good handymen, and anglers who are should be able to make most of the types of spoons and spinners that are produced commercially. There is great scope for inventiveness, both artistic and scientific, in the making of artificial lures, and with today's materials available we feel there are many new types waiting for an active mind and skilful hands: or if not new basic types, at least new faces on old lures.

Let's begin with the household dessert spoon. Although this is often talked about, it is unusual to see anglers using a home-made Copper and Silver style spoon. Yet they are easy to construct and highly efficient. In the first place many dessert spoons have the correct egg-shaped outline with the correct convexity, and it is easy to find them in different qualities or weights of metal. Firstly, saw off the handle with a hacksaw, then use a file to round off that end of the spoon. Alternatively, the next step can be done first, namely, drilling a hole at each end of the spoon: if you do this drilling first you can hang on to the spoon handle whilst doing so. Make the holes with a diameter of about 2-3 mm, but not too far from the ends: the nearest edge of each hole should be about 2 mm from the end of the finished spoon. If this last distance is made any greater it is almost impossible to fit split rings without straining them.

Split rings are a problem. Quite simply, look for strength and smallness. Those where the wire has a flattened cross-section and a little kink or two where the ends meet tend to be weak: these should only be used on small spinners and in the smaller sizes. Having obtained good split rings, attach one to each hole of the spoon. Then to the narrow end (opposite the 'handle' end) add a swivel, and to the broad end a treble hook. In the case of really large spoons it's a good idea to add a treble to the front end too, and it doesn't seem to impair the action of the lure unduly. The only remaining problem is to colour it. A whole suite of perfectly good spoons can be made in this fashion.

But in general it is necessary to cut the spoon blades you need from sheet metal, simply because you may wish to make long Jim Vincents, concavo-convex spoons and so on. Almost all metals are useful at times. What you must do is keep a sharp eye open for bits of metal everywhere — tin trays, reflectors from car lamps, bumpers, and many other everyday discarded items can be used. Alternatively, it is possible to buy quite small sheets of different metals of varying weights.

First, you need to get a really good shape cut out in cardboard so that you can place it on the metal sheet and pencil around it. We always get someone to cut out ours with the right equipment, since labouring away with a hacksaw can be really hard work and not very accurate. Having got the right outline it is necessary to file down any bumps or rough edges, before attempting to shape the curve of the blade. For this

21 Barrie's work-bench, with some spinner-making tools and materials.

22 Cutting a spinner to shape.

purpose you need a round-headed hammer or two, and a large block of wood such as a cross-section of tree about two feet across. A shoemaker's last is also useful. The effect of the hammering is to produce a bumpy or scale-like finish which is no bad thing on a spoon. When first trying to hammer out a flat piece of metal into a convex spoon of the Jim Vincent style, it is easy to become enthusiastic and quickly ruin its shape. Begin tentatively until you see how that particular piece of metal is responding to the hammer. In time you will find that it is quite easy to make a shallowly convex spoon, or a deeply convex one, or a concavo-convex one.

Perhaps the most common mistake made by beginners at this game is to use metal that is too thin, simply because it can be cut very easily with tin-snips. Tin-snips are useful, and they come in different strengths and sizes, but it is advisable to find someone with good metalwork equipment who will cut out your shapes for you. Having got your shape ready, and having hammered it to the required convexity, all that is needed are the finishing touches that you made to the C & S spoon discussed above.

Bar-spoons are a little bit more tricky. You'll need the same equipment as for spoons, but in addition a good pair of long-nosed pliers with rounded jaws; metal wire for the axial wire; dress eyes (from pairs of hook and eyes) for attaching blades to the bar; beads, and bodies (or weights) for the bar.

The first step is to prepare the blade itself in the same way as for spoons, but remember that the metal can be much lighter and in this case is easily cut with snips. Drill a hole at *one* end in exactly the same way as with spoons, but do *not* thread the blade on the bar wire. If you do this the blade is too close to the bar and to any body or weight that you place on it, and it does not rotate efficiently. Instead, modify a dress eye as shown in Fig. G (or use a commercial device), put the blade on this, and then thread the dress eyes on to the bar. This means the whole blade attachment swings much more loosely although, of course, quite securely.

23 Beating the spinner to obtain curve.

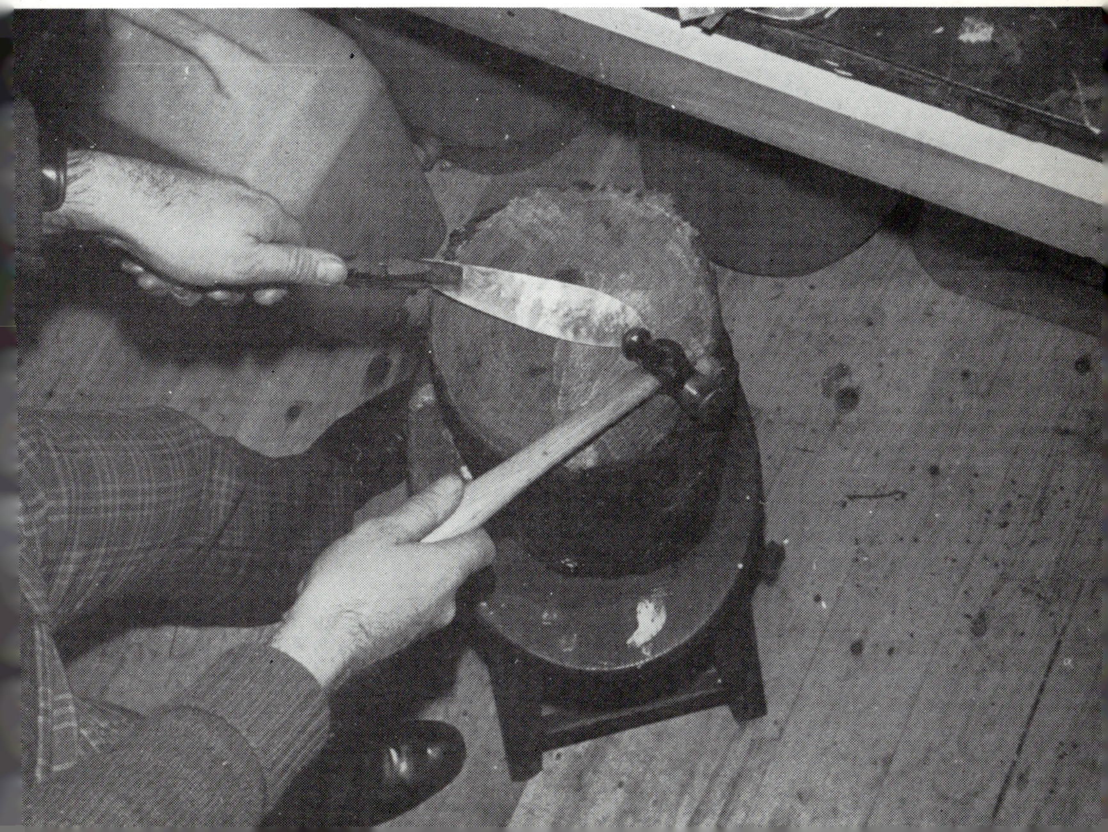

The tricky bit with bar-spoons comes just before you add the blade to the bar. It is necessary to bend the bar wire into a ring at the front end (Fig. G) and to do this use either the long-nosed pliers, or a thin metal rod firmly clamped in a vice. You need a neat round ring, and whilst this is easy to achieve with soft wire such a ring is useless in a spinner since it bends the first time you cast it into a piece of bridgework. The wire needed is stainless steel piano or music wire in various grades. Sizes 24 and 26 are two useful thicknesses, and ours comes in 1 lb weights from Ibbotsons of Sheffield. It is tough stuff, and you're sure to suffer a lacerated finger or two before the evening is out.

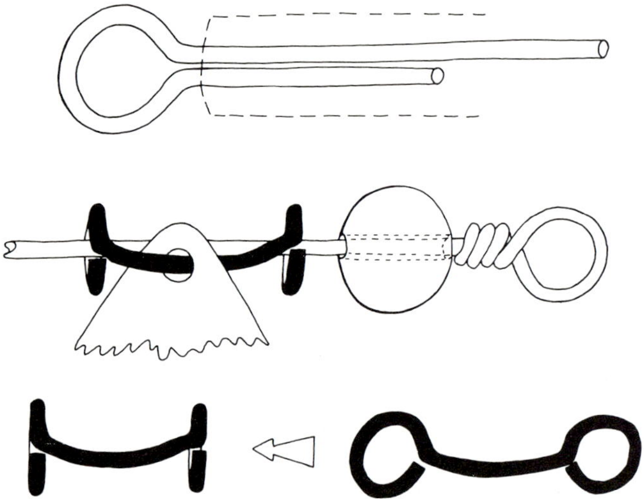

Fig. **G**

Having constructed a loop as shown in Fig. G, slide a bead along the bar so that it is flush up to the loop, then add the blade itself, then another bead; at which point you must decide whether to have a body of beads, plastic tube, swan shots, barrel lead, dowel rod, or what-have-you. When you have the body in place, add another bead, and finally make a loop at the end on which to add a split ring and treble hook. Do not jam the whole lot up too tight so that the dress eye cannot rotate. In our experience the body is best glued in position so that wear, tear and breakage is not caused by the assembly forever sliding up and down the bar.

The first bar-spoons that Ray Webb and Barrie made for use on Hornsea Mere looked extremely crude, worked like a bomb, and on the first trip to Hornsea took a blind pike of three pounds, which surely proves that the vibrations were right! At this stage it is possible to experiment with bar length, blade shapes, body weights and so on. The only thing to watch is that the bigger you make them the more difficult it is to make them work well. For the larger sizes we copy the proprietary brands such as Vibro. Incidentally a number of firms, Tom Saville's included, make a whole range of spinner-maker's accessories including the eyelets and beads, so that by being inventive and shopping around as well, the would-be spinning enthusiast is well catered for (see Photo. 24).

It is not our intention to give a blow-by-blow account of making all sorts of spinners, since our two descriptions cover a great range of lures once the basic principles are mastered, but we shall briefly give a pointer

24 A selection of materials obtainable from Tom Saville's tackle shop at Nottingham.

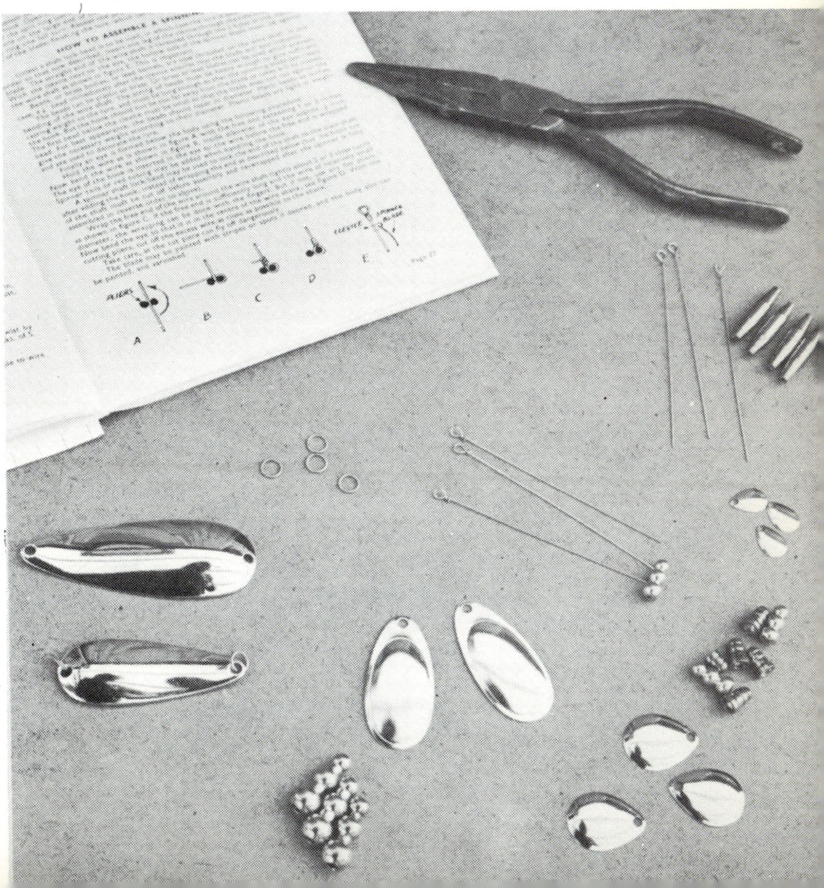

or two towards some of the other types of spinner. Quill minnows, for example, are best made by actually buying one of the type that you fancy, or which is very good on your waters, and then copying it at home. You'll need cable wire, bird quills in various diameters, treble hooks, whipping thread and varnish. Traditionally, tapered shank trebles are used in quill minnows and these are certainly less cumbersome than eyed trebles which will suffice for the rest of home spinner making.

Mackerel spinners are difficult unless you have access to facilities for brazing a tube along the centre of the blade. This tube *can* be Araldited into position, but the life of the spinner is shorter. The rest of a mackerel spinner is easy once you have this problem mastered. Wagtails need very little comment since today there is a wide range of rubber and plastic tubing available. Apart from this you'll need cabled wire, beads etc., and some thin metal from which to make the spinning vanes at the head end. The only difficulty is fixing these vanes to a rigid head at the front of the lure. Again Araldite, the universal cure-all, stick-all, is necessary. Wooden minnows and metal minnows can be made if you can use wood- and metal-turning lathes and drilling equipment, but wooden minnows can, at a pinch, be made without this equipment.

All that is needed then, for all the above concoctions, is polishing up, finishing off, and a coat of paint in places. But just how important *is* shine and colour, and where should it be? We carried out some brief experiments in flume tanks. The results were interesting and we give an account of them in the following paragraphs.

Spinner action and colours

The series of photographs accompanying this section show the light patterns made by spinners as they would probably appear to a fish. Lighting was set up over the tank to represent natural sunlight on a sunny day — lighting was not rigged to simulate winter conditions during any of the tests applied. To ensure that the camera recorded the pictures seen as a fish would see the lure, a neutral background was erected, which did not make the light patterns stand out in any way. In fact, the neutral colour as nearly represented a distant blank wall of water as was possible.

A current of approximately 2 knots was fed through the tank to represent a slow river or stream. The camera was set at right-angles to, and level with the lure, and a set of three photographs of each one was

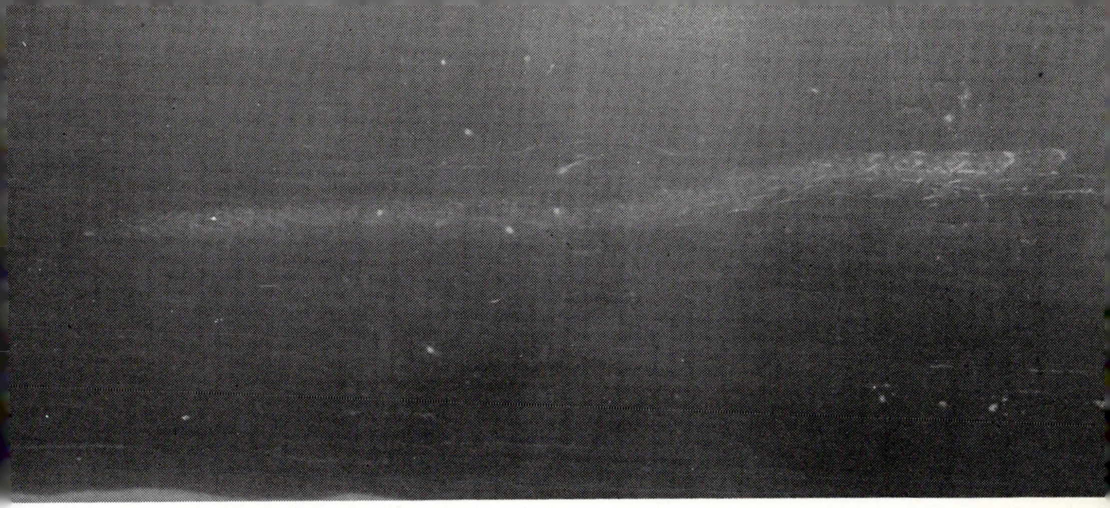

25 Patterns from the Mepps Rainbo.

taken, the first two with an open shutter speed of one second, and the spinner moved across the plane of the lens during this time. The third was a one-second exposure with the lure held steady, only the current moving the spinner. The water in the tank was clear, eighteen inches deep, over a rippled clean sand bottom. Perhaps we should say a word or two about the tank itself. Thanks to the help of one of Barrie's colleagues, Peter Friend, we were able to use what is called a flume tank. In this case it was about ten yards long, a couple of feet deep, about eighteen inches wide, and the current controllable within wide limits. The flow is laminar, rather than turbulent, and is more akin to a long sweep of river or drain with a steady depth than, for example, the turbulence of a weir pool, or a series of pools on a small river.

26 Abu Toby patterns.

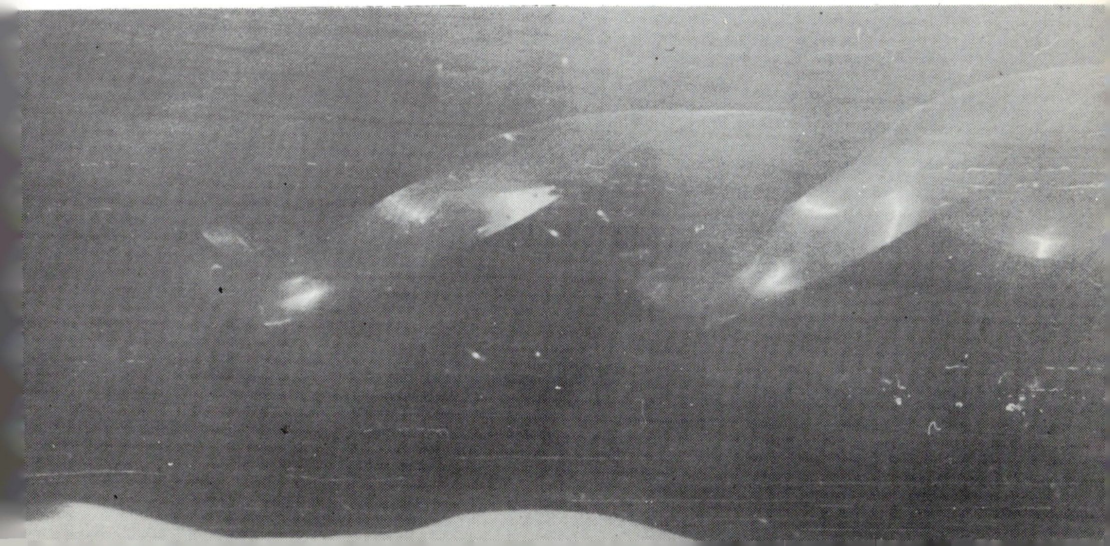

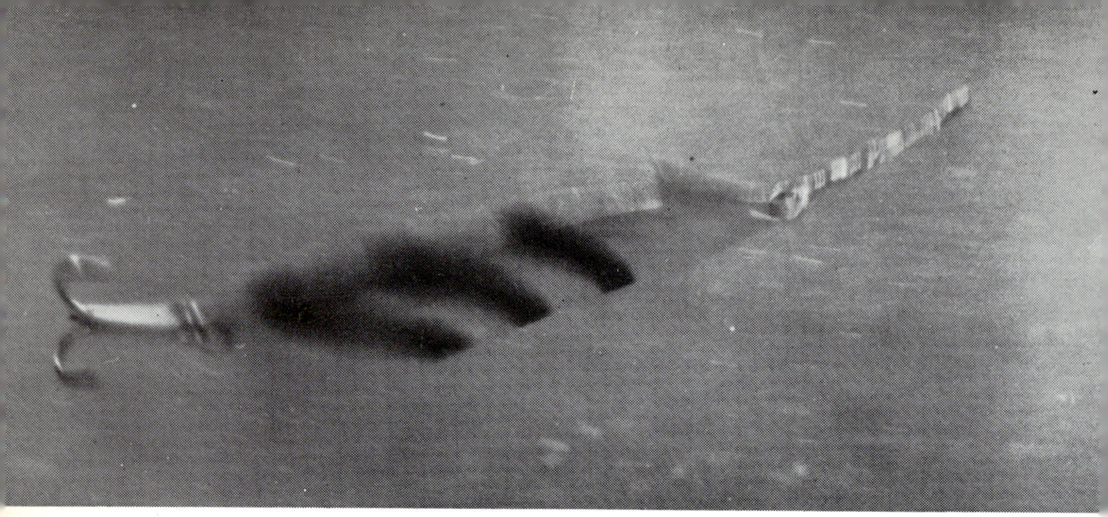

27 Patterns from a Piker Spoon.

What a fish can see is, of course, open to some debate. Most zoologists, and beyond question most anglers, take the view that fish see colours quite well. Equally likely is that some fish, like pike, rely heavily on vibrations rather than sight, particularly in coloured water, whereas perch often give the impression to the spinning man of possessing really good eyesight. Be that as it may it is certainly possible, though perhaps unlikely, that each flick of a spoon or twirl of a spinner is seen clearly by the fish as a succession of sharp images. More likely, we feel, is that the hunting fish sees, and feels the vibrations of, an elongated disturbed area. What it sees is a series of flashes, and what it feels is a series of pulses on its lateral line sense organs. When we viewed the spinner in action from the sides of our tank that is exactly what *we* saw, and the

28 Light patterns from the Mepps Mino.

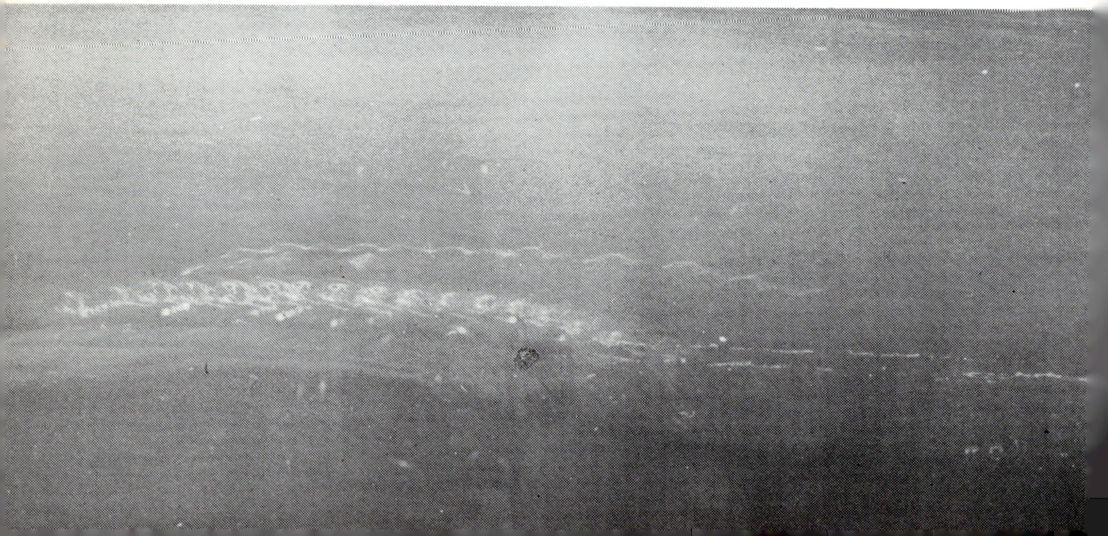

human eye is pretty good. So that most of our photographs, with an open shutter speed of one second, illustrate the light pattern characteristic of those spinners, and what we feel the fish actually sees in most circumstances.

Some interesting observations were made. Ondex bar-spoons for example, superb killers on Fenland drains and shallow lakes, actually have very little flash pattern and what did occur came from the 'upper' end of the revolving blade and would not readily be seen by fish on the bottom. This spinner, and some others such as Veltics, are very good vibrating lures, and it may well be that the fish home in on the vibrations, and then by sight on the red tag tail which most of them carry. Obviously then, you would use this type of spinner when you needed vibrations or a dull spinner.

The Mepps Rainbo, in contrast, sent out a constant light pattern of a tight circle (Photo. 25) from the multi-reflecting surface of the willow-leaf blade; the non-reflective underside breaking the pattern to give a light-and-dark effect that would be visible for some distance and over quite a wide arc of view.

Both Toby and Piker spoons, large lures in red and silver, show a striking figure-of-eight pattern (Photos. 26 and 27) that reflects light on the top edge (the shoulder of the bait). Only a few turns have been made in the same distance that the Mepps would make many, but the pattern is both clearly visible over a wide area and striking in nature. As already mentioned, the Toby actually spins strongly in more powerful currents. Both show a typical tail-down position when retrieved slowly, but experience shows us that this is not unattractive to the hunting fish.

Colorado spinners showed the least light pattern of any we tried, and the red inside blocked what little light there was at every turn. Nor are vibrations very strong from this lure, yet we have caught hundreds of good perch on the smaller sizes, and good lough pike on the big sizes — which suggests that there could be other factors involved in its value as a spinner.

The Mepps Mino gave a small, tight light pattern though not so pronounced as with the Rainbo. Most of the light reflects off the *edges* of the revolving blade, and some off the plastic minnow which can be seen as a grey hue under the main light pattern of the spinner (Photo. 28). This seemed the most effective of the gold coloured lures that we tried.

Our Russian weedless spoons, in effect two spoons mounted face to face (Photo. 38(2)) gave light reflections from the shoulders of *each* blade, but produced a show visible only over a short distance. Vibrations

29 Piker Spoon patterns.

nil: definitely a spoon for bright conditions if we are to accept the concept of bright lure for dull conditions and *vice versa*.

The general conclusion that we came to was that light patterns turn off the edge and shoulders of a lure as it revolves or wobbles. In terms of flash, the small leaf bar-spoons and Jim Vincent-type wobbling spoons are undoubtedly best. Round lures like the Colorado, and the large rounded blades as in the Ondex, do not show up well. Many of the red, gold and black blobs may count for nothing in the fishes' eyes once the lure is revolving. Coloured bars, on the other hand, *do* influence the light patterns strongly, the best being those that run obliquely or horizontally from nose to tail, breaking up the glint of the lure into quicker patterns. The 'stationary' photograph (Photo. 27) of the Piker spoon shows this quite clearly. Multi-reflecting surfaces on lures of any sort will obviously increase show. It seems a pity that none is yet on spoons in the really large sizes. Clearly, considerable thought is needed when painting your home-made spoons, the construction of which is outlined in the first part of this chapter. The main problem concerns spots and blobs — are they really necessary?

8

Natural baits

Spun and wobbled deadbaits are undoubtedly the most neglected methods of fishing in the whole of the sport, particularly the former. Probably the aftermath of the Victorians has something to do with it — people immediately conjure up a picture of several hundredweights of ironmongery in the form of hooks, swivels and gimp wire, garnished with evil-smelling preserved baits that slop into and taint everything within view. But ideas have changed and methods with them, and those old evils are now as dead as the Dodo.

There are several very good reasons for using a deadbait, the first of which is directly connected with size. Earlier in the book we lamented the passing of the really heavy spoon or spinner that could cover areas of water which the modern lightweights cannot reach or descend into. With a deadbait the most distant river bank is the limit, the only thing that could possibly govern the size of bait selected being the strength and ability of both the angler and his rod. In progressing upwards into light beachcasting tackle there is no real bar to size. Even on those enormous gravel pits where boats are forbidden, the angler armed with a large spun or wobbled deadbait and matching tackle is the only person who is equipped to fish water that others cannot — or will not — reach.

Cheapness is another concrete reason for using the deadbait. As we shall see later in this chapter, it is not necessary to use elaborate or expensive rigs, so the man with his deadbait can take financial risks by fishing weeded or snag-ridden areas where a brother angler, armed with his £1-a-throw spinner, cannot, or dare not fish.

But it is the versatility of the deadbait, its ease of control, the ultra slow wobble, part-wobble or spinning action which practically induces the bait to talk that produces fish when use of the artificial may fail.

Deep-freezing has made deadbait spinning child's play. We have both cultivated our local fishmongers who allow us to select the herrings, mackerel and sprats that we want and by bulk-buying and individually freezing each fish we are able to stock twice a year or so with first-rate baits. We not only take care that our fish is fresh but also are careful to be selective in size and weight so that we don't damage our tackle with occasional block-busters that strain rods or snap the line during the cast.

30 Distance with ease, using a wobbled deadbait.

Shock leaders, 10 feet or so of nylon monofilament of a much greater breaking strain than the line attached to the rest of the reel, can obviate quite a lot of strain and prevent the dangerous accident of snapping off during a cast. Generally, however, these are not necessary. Believe us — a large dead fish loaded with umpteen large trebles flying through the air can be dangerous, both to the angler and the occasional spectator. There is also the tragic possibility of a water bird or stray household pet animal

31 Snags galore! Best dealt with by a spun deadbait for the pocket's sake.

attempting to eat the lost bait. Rare though such an event must be, it is of such stuff that propaganda is made for the anti-anglers brigade.

We also freeze any sizeable freshwater fish that we can, their flesh being firmer and less likely to split during a cast than sea fish. But somehow we never seem able to put enough away, possibly because of our livebaiting demands.

There is no doubt that the toughest and most long-lasting bait for spinning is one that has been preserved, and for the benefit of those anglers who are already wrinkling up their noses with the imagined smell of formalin on reading these words, we set out our method of preserving that leaves no taint, no smell, and produces a first-rate bait in its natural colours.

Add a pint of water to a tablespoonful of 40 per cent formaldehyde, obtainable from a chemist. Place the baits in this, and leave them for two days. At the end of this time they should be carefully washed in cold water, and the formaldehyde solution thrown away. Take care to wipe any greasy film from the baits, and then place them into a mixture of one part of sugar in four parts of water, using a wide-necked jar or open pan of some sort. After a few days exposed to the air in this, the taint of formaldehyde will have disappeared. They can now be packed into a Kilner jar, a fresh brew of four parts water to one of sugar poured over them, and the jar sealed. They will keep for as long as you want, and be as attractive to use as when they were first killed. One word of warning — formaldehyde is poisonous. Be sure to wash everything that you use thoroughly, do not leave the mixture lying around within the reach of children, and make sure you wash your hands after every part of the operation.

The search for firm baits has led us to try some pretty odd things in our time, but one of the latest methods we have adopted is undoubtedly the best. We start by thoroughly drying any fish, whether from the deep-freeze, the fishmonger's slab or the preserving jar, with an old towel. When they are as dry as possible, we dip them into a medium-sized tin of clear cellulose varnish (Ronseal clear is one of our favourites) and then hang them up to dry (see Photo. 32). Those baits too large to fit completely into the tin we dunk as far as possible, and then paint them with a brush so that a thick skin of varnish dries from nose to tail.

We only do enough baits for one day's fishing in this way — they don't last any longer — and prepare them in the shed on the day before we fish. By adding yellow Dylon dye to the varnish we can turn out golden baits, or we may use any other colour that we feel we might need. In fact

32 Sealing sprats.

it is possible to make golden and natural coloured baits by part dipping or painting. The permutations are endless, and our finished baits are firm enough to withstand really hard usage.

Quite how our ancestors managed to tote deadbaits around before the marketing of Tuppaware we do not know. We have several different sizes of these boxes that we pack baits into before leaving home, including a few ready mounted on whatever rig we are going to need. More especially do we do this where really large baits, which take time to mount, are to be used: the early casts made at the beginning of a day are often the most productive, so it is essential that precious minutes are not wasted.

As to the mounts that we use — well, starting with the smallest and simplest, we have the treble-mounted minnow. There is a special tool that makes mounting this lightweight child's play; just a darning bodkin pushed into a wooden handle so that the eyed end is outwards. It takes seconds to slide this through the mouth and body of the minnow, then

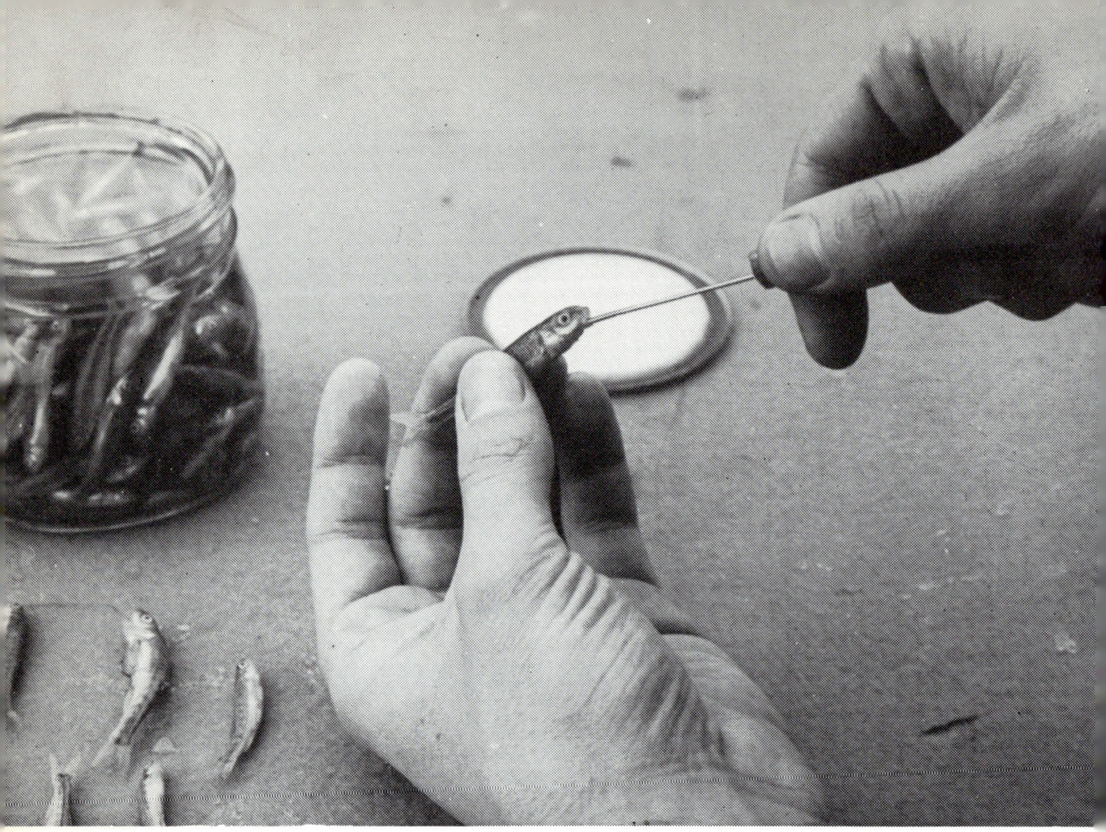

33 Mounting minnows with a darning needle.

out through the vent. A short length of nylon with size 12 or smaller trebles (depending on bait size) ready tied on is then threaded through the bodkin eye and pulled back out through the mouth taking the line with it (see Photo. 33). Simple but very effective. Split shot can be pinched on to the cast loosely, and slid down into the mouth to provide any necessary weight to help control the retrieve. Cast from an ultra-light rod with a very fine line it makes just about the most killing bait we know for chub, perch, trout and, often, pike.

By the time one or two casts have been made with this rig the vent end of the minnow will have worked well down around the bend of the treble, causing it to swerve and wobble in large circles. If you want to keep its original wobbling action, that of small circles, then try using a single sliced hook instead of the treble. Pull the shank well up into the belly, and it will hold the bait firmly in place. The difference in action that this makes is quite considerable.

Bleak and sprats are superb spinners mounted on a sprat mount —

leaded, with vanes and three trebles (Photos. 34(1) and 35). Although they are moderately priced one can make them, using sheet plastic for the vanes, a baiting needle and barrel lead for the body pin and cabled Alasticum with suitable trebles. For fishing shallow water where weight would possibly be a disadvantage, use a prawn mount, which is identical in every way except that there is no lead weight on the body pin. Quite often we have seen sprats mounted on both these rigs by anglers who insist on putting a kink in the body of the bait. This merely destroys the spinning action imparted by the vanes, and produces a wobble. Mount the bait absolutely straight for a perfect spin, and remove the vanes completely and mount with the body curved if you are seeking a wobble action.

Probably the quickest and cheapest way of mounting a wobbling sprat is with the double hook steel pin, shown in Photos. 34(2) and 35. These cost a few pence each, can be pushed through the body and clipped on to the eye mount, then attached to the line or trace. It isn't always necessary to push the pin from vent to mouth — if the pin is pushed out

34 1. Mounted sprat — sprat and prawn tackle. 2. Sprat mounted on two hook bait pin.

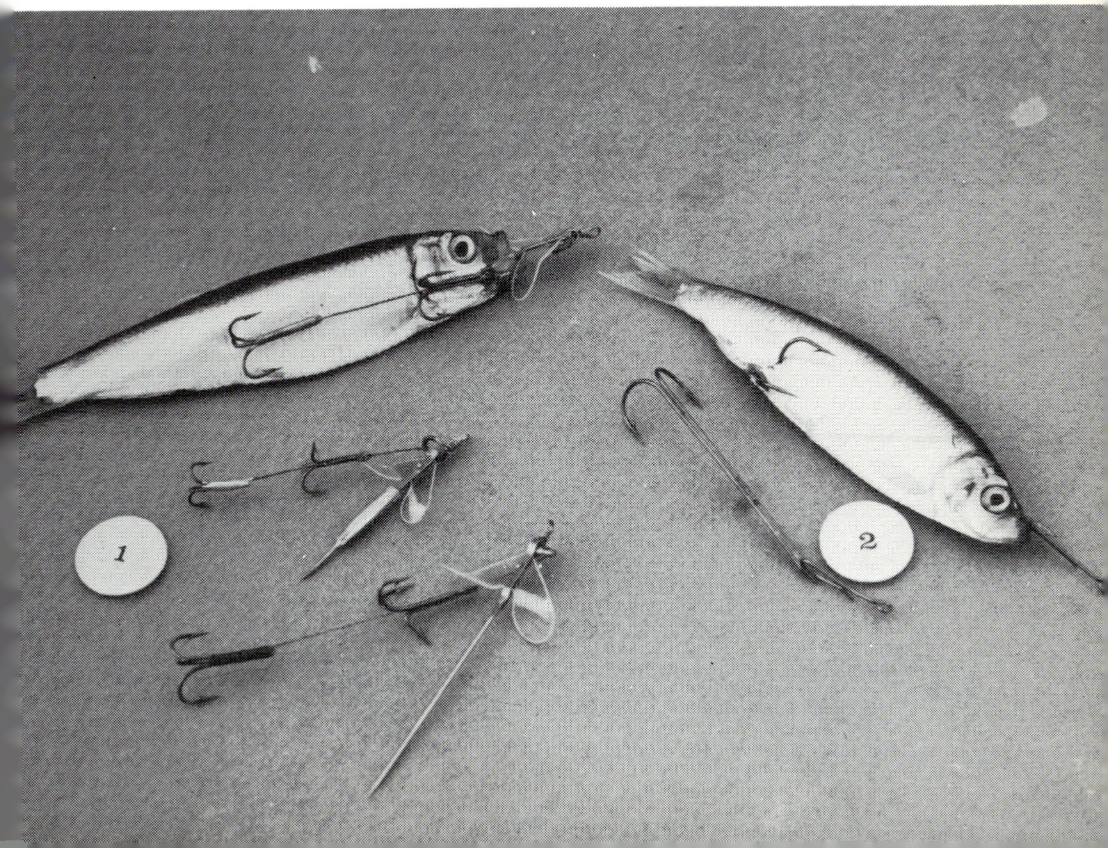

just behind the gill then the set angle will make the bait take on a first-rate wide sweeping curve that we have found irresistible to pike. If there is any disadvantage in this method it is that lead for weighting must be placed on to the cast and not inside the fish. This may seem a very small point, but the difference between cast and body weighting is reflected in any action which the angler may attempt to induce into the bait by raising or lowering the rod, or shifting the angle of retrieve from one side of the body to the other. This is immediately transferred to the lead on the cast, as opposed to the bait, when the lead is carried externally.

When it comes to rigs for larger deadbaits such as herrings, large roach etc., there is a lot to be said for the Jardine snap tackle for a mount when one is casting over short distances. The end treble is pushed well below the dorsal fin, pulling the tail back to produce a wobble action. The second treble should be pointed into the shoulder, behind the gill cover. The end of the trace is slid under the gill and out through the mouth so that strain during both cast and retrieve travels through the bait, not to the outside hooks. Two or three turns of fine nylon round the shoulder

35 DEADBAIT TACKLES. 1 & 2. Plastic imitation minnows. 3. Double-hook baiting pin. 4. Sprat spinner. 5. Prawn spinner. 6. Archer flight.

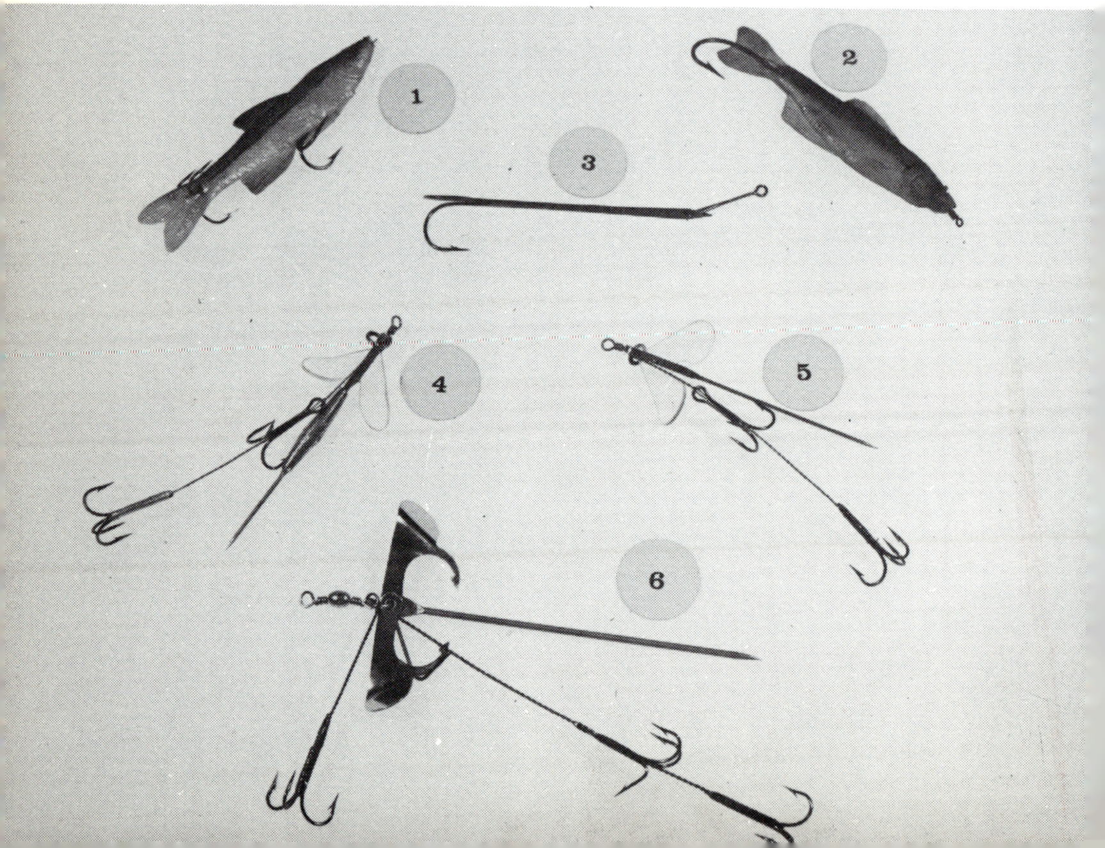

of the bait will also help to hold it on to the hooks, and a small barrel lead can be slid down the trace into the mouth to provide body weight.

For long-distance casting the bait must be mounted so that it holds together, and cannot break apart either during the cast, on impact with the water, or during the retrieve. It is still possible to obtain Archer Deadbait spinning mounts (Photo. 36) and as a spinning rig this takes a lot of beating. Both metal vanes open outwards, the body pin is pushed through the mouth, and head of the bait slid between the jaws. Both vanes are then closed and the head and body hooks are fastened into place. Our photo shows one set of trebles — those on the other side of the body being hidden.

We add any extra weight that may be needed to the body pin by means of barrel leads or, if we want to cover shallow water, air is injected into the stomach with a hypodermic syringe. Incidentally, if we are going to use the air treatment we take care to push the body pin upwards into the flesh below the backbone so that the stomach will remain unpunctured.

For large baits that are to be wobbled we find nothing to beat the single big treble threaded from vent to mouth. During the threading it is an advantage if you pass the baiting needle out through the flank for about an inch or so, then back into the centre of the body (see Photo. 36). This helps to create a shallow curve in the bait during the retrieve and also helps to keep it from collapsing back on the rear treble.

Actually, this collapsing problem where the points on the end treble finish up buried into the vent of the bait can prevent the hooks getting a good grip when a strike is made. We have both lost fish because of it, and at the moment are experimenting with small buttons or washers threaded on the Alasticum immediately above the eye of the treble before it is mounted, to act as a buffer between it and the flesh. Our early results have been good, and our hooking ratio to strikes made has shown a distinct improvement. Other anglers use a split polythene tube of about $\frac{3}{4}$-inch length, convex side outwards.

Of course, there are many more rigs that one can use for mounting natural baits for both spinning or wobbling — Fred Buller's book *Pike* shows an excellent selection — but we have described only those that we use. They are all very simple, and it is this very simplicity that has endeared them to us. The more trebles and Alasticum that attaches to a rig, the greater the difficulty in mounting the bait. Not only that, but we are entirely unconvinced that pure numbers of hooks are any better at holding a fish, or even increasing one's chances of hooking them when the strike is made. But, as we stated at the beginning of this chapter, this

36 MOUNTED HERRINGS. 1. Archer rig. 2. Adapted Jardine-snap. 3. Single treble, body threaded.

is an under-exploited section of the spinner's craft, and it is wide open to experiment. There is no doubt that the perfect rig or mount has yet to be invented.

Our earlier mention of flexibility when retrieving a natural bait deserves a little enlargement. We notice that most spinning enthusiasts who take to using dead fish still imagine that they are towing a lump of metal through the water, and whether it is because they subconsciously fear that by slowing the bait it will not spin correctly or, worse, will catch on the bottom, they continue to retrieve at far too fast a rate. Quite apart from its natural attraction, the whole idea of using a dead fish as a lure is because any buoyancy that it possesses will keep it fishing when other baits collapse and sink. It is impossible to retrieve a wobbled bait too slowly — in fact, we occasionally stop and deliberately allow any we are using to drop to the bottom, often taking a fish as the bait slides slowly downwards. At its slowest, wobbled deadbaiting is only one step removed from static deadbaiting.

Retrieving a spun deadbait demands a slow even retrieve that should be practised in the water at one's feet until the slowest movement consistent with the bait's turning is established. Beware of sudden snatching at any time, regardless of whether you are spinning or wobbling. This can only tear hooks out of the flesh, or worse, cause the skin of the bait to break up. Of course, there's no reason why a change of pace should not be made; just avoid snatching.

Finally, we would like to remove all reservations that exist in anglers' minds that natural baits can only be fished for pike, and only then on large waters. Spun sprats and minnows are acknowledged as killing baits for salmon and trout respectively, whilst a spun bleak is the bait *par excellence* for Thames trout. Perch and chub are very partial to all these baits, particularly minnow at any time of the year. As for the size of water one fishes — well, even in the smallest brook a dead fish is more easily controlled than a metal spinner or spoon, capable, with careful weighting, of working into tight corners where the artificial just cannot begin to function. Add to this our previous point of cheapness and the

37 The shirt-button stopper, keeping the treble from jamming into the body.

case for a working natural bait makes a great deal of sense. The actual techniques of retrieving spun and wobbled deadbaits will be dealt with in the sections appropriate to the relevant species. Suffice it to say for the present that with spun deadbaits, which are usually smaller than wobbled deadbaits, the strike is instant: with small wobbled deadbaits this can also apply, but in general the angler should steel himself to treat each tiny pluck as a good take and then stop retrieving and wait for the fish to move off with the bait.

PART THREE
Techniques

9

Techniques of spinning

The techniques of spinning are as varied as in any other branch of angling, if not more so. Spinners can be pulled fast through the surface waves, bouncing from wave to wave; retrieved slow and deep; held static, but spinning, in fast currents; and Barrie has actually had two pike, small ones, take a spinner in the air some 4-5 inches above the surface of the water, although he wouldn't recommend this as a regularly producing technique! The idea in spinning is to have spinners or methods to cover as many contingencies as possible: there's no point in having a box of mackerel spinners if you are fishing the River Shannon, for example, where a few big Copper and Silvers would be better, coupled with a powerful two-handed rod and fifteen lb b.s. line.

On the other hand we do not subscribe to the view that you can do almost anything with a spinner that can be done with a natural bait. There are many occasions when natural baits, whether spun, wobbled or static, will outscore a spinner. And in general, spinning is less effective in winter than in summer. For the salmon family this is, of course, no problem, but in pike, perch, zander and chub fishing it is as well to remember that when the water temperature gets really low a small natural bait is more likely to effect their capture.

That then is the first major point of this section, that spinning in the warmer months is not only more pleasant, it is usually more effective. We cannot emphasize too strongly that the movement involved in spinning is insufficient to keep an angler warm in really cold weather, and it is an old wives' tale to suppose otherwise. This is not to say that we do no spinning in winter. On the contrary, in fact, but we choose the conditions carefully, and the waters carefully. In every area of the country you will find waters which, sometimes for no obvious reason, respond well to artificials in winter.

The other aspect of *when* to spin is what time of the day or night. The answer is anytime, whatever you are fishing for. Pike, for example, home in quite happily to a vibrating spinner in pitch darkness, just as small brownies will do on a mountain stream. As we pointed out in chapters 6 & 7, vibrations are probably all-important in lure location by the fish. Personally, we do not mind fishing in the heat of a summer's day, provided it is the kind of leisurely affair that one indulges in after a morning's tench fishing. But in general the dawn, dusk, and night periods tend to be best, just as they are for so much fishing.

When spinning at night it is as well to have a small Billy Lane stop knot, tied in nylon, on your line about 10 feet above the lure: this gives a little click as it enters your top ring and tells you that your lure is 10 feet away from the bank or rod tip. In addition, you must be careful to have at the top of the trace something that is big enough to be stopped by the top ring of the rod. The last thing you want to happen is to have the trace swivel or spinner link swivel enter the end eye of the rod: you can stop it with a swan shot, or bead, or some types of anti-kink vanes.

Another useful trick is to have a stop of sorts at the *other* end of the line, which tells you how far you have cast. In this case it is not possible, or at least not sensible, to use a Billy Lane stop knot since this tends to cause tangles when buried on the spool. But having decided how far you wish to cast, say 30 yards, pull off that amount of line, then add a thin rubber band to the spool, and finally reel back on the 30 yards of line. On casting, the whole lot pulls up short when 30 yards of line are out. This is useful when the casts are made regularly across and down a river that is, say, 35 yards wide. On occasions when there is just enough visibility, you soon get used to making casts of variable length and direction. Otherwise night spinning is as easy as during the day, and is merely a matter of knowing where everything is. Netting a fish is usually a matter of netting the splashes, and things can occasionally go a little awry here, but if you can get the fish sliding bankwards after judging the distance of the splashes the problems are few. It is possible to tape a small torch on the handle of the net, just about a foot above the net rim. Switching on a torch can affect your own night vision for a few minutes, but a little light at the actual moment of netting can be helpful. Night spinning is exciting, and more than in any other aspect of the sport the take seems to come thumping out of nowhere. You develop a sense of feel and touch that you didn't realise you had, almost to the extent that you get from worming mountain streams for brownies in the dark.

So far we have considered when to spin, and the general effects of weather and temperature, but another important matter is *where* to spin. Here there are really no restrictions other than those placed by club rules. Large reservoirs and huge rivers like the Shannon or the Great Ouse Relief Channel can be imposing, and the natural tendency is to use big lures and powerful tackle, partly in order to cover the water and partly to give you the feeling that at least the fish has *seen* it. But in fact, light spinning on big waters can be extremely productive at times, and the only things wrong with big waters are the air of monotony that they manage to convey, and your own sense of feeling very puny while flicking out a tiny Mepps spinner into a vast emptiness.

Almost all waters can be spun through, including snaggy and weedy water, and before going on to some general matters concerning what one might term standard spinning technique, we shall say a word or two about that special situation of fishing in the weed or snags. The problem is twofold really: firstly, the link swivel or top trace swivel gets caught in soft blanket or silk weed, as do the trebles; secondly, the hooks themselves easily foul coarser weed, logs and so on. The first of these problems is almost insoluble since blanket weed will clog anything, but other weeds and snags can be defeated to some extent by using weed guards on the treble hooks. These are easily constructed from SWG wire of the appropriate grade (in this case no. 28 SWG) and such a spinner can be retrieved through sunken trees and water lilies with little fear of snagging up. After a few outings the weed guards become strained and need to be reset or replaced by new ones. Weed guards of this type can be used on any trebles, and if not too rigid will not impede the striking qualities of the lure.

Another idea is shown in Photo. 38, which illustrates a Russian spoon consisting of two lightly sprung blades. On a take, the blades are pushed together exposing the hooks simultaneously. Barrie first used these lures on a Peterborough brick pit where he and Fred Wagstaffe fished them without loss through huge sunken trees and masses of branches. As spoons, they are not as effective at attracting fish since their action is rather lifeless, but it should not be beyond the imagination of inventive anglers to produce a home-made lure on the same principle, which does work well.

A third way of beating weeds is to use a lure such as the Bushwhacker (Fig. E on page 47). These are a sort of combined spoon/spinner/fly and they fish really well through lily beds, branches, and even *Potamogeton* beds. As with all lures, they give up the ghost in really soft weed.

Many anglers are realizing that great sport can be had by looking for fish *in* weedbeds as opposed to fishing the fringes, and it may be that other weed-defeating ideas will come out in the future. In the meantime, apart from the above ideas, various commercially made lures have excellent built-in weed guards. The use of big single hooks may increase for such fishing, since it is easier to build a good weed guard for one hook than to make three for a treble hook.

Homing in now to general spinning technique, we shall assume that, as already recommended, you will have the appropriate tackle for your water. On that assumption we'll go on to think about the following topics: still waters from the bank; rivers from the bank; and still waters from a boat — digressing at times to interpose related matters of tackle or technique. At an early stage the angler will decide on a wire trace or not, and for pike and zander there really should be no question: as thin and as dark a trace as possible is the ideal, in a breaking strain not dissimilar to that of the reel line. For other species the reel line can be tied directly to the spinner eye or to a link swivel to facilitate changing of lure during the day. In the last instance you need to be confident of your knot for a day's spinning.

38 WEEDLESS SPINNERS. 1. Abu Flamingo. 2. Russian Double-spoon. 3. Mepps Aglia — single hook. 4. Abu Reflex Vass.

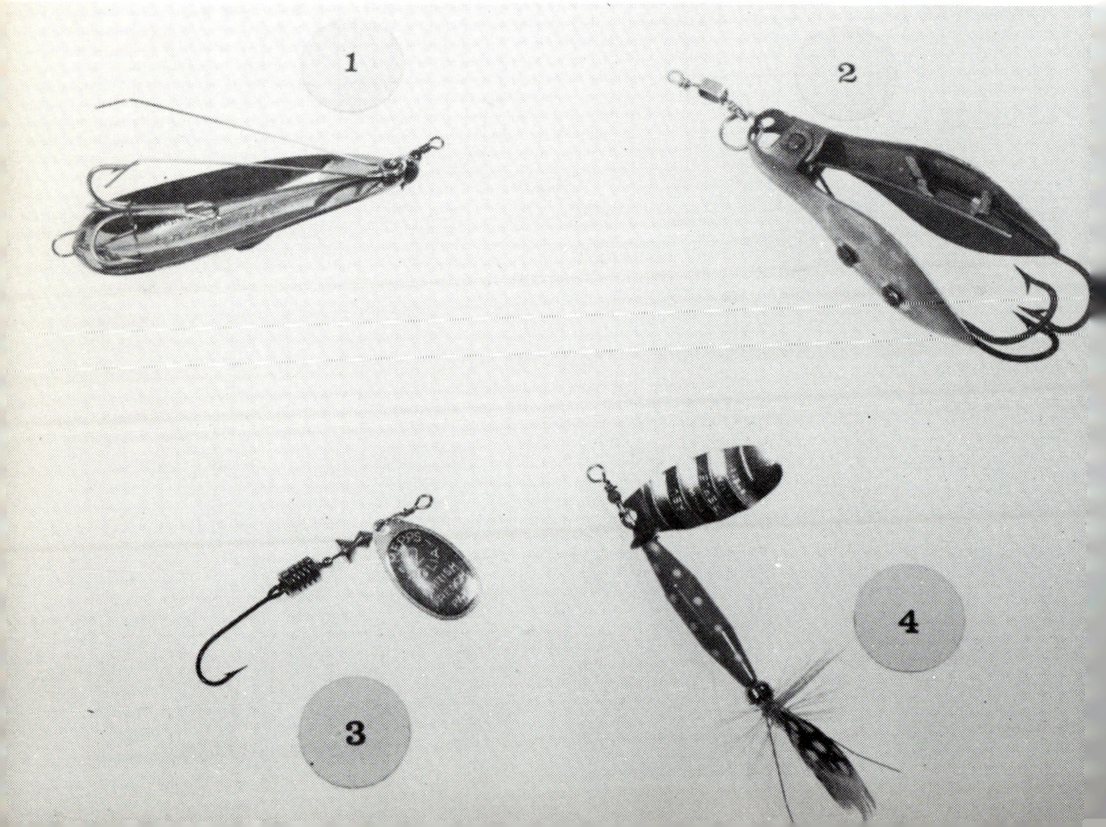

This brings us to the question of using an anti-kink vane. We discussed the various types in chapter 4, and it really boils down to whether the angler is prepared to risk kinks in his line. Personally we do not like encumbrances on the line, and a bit of light spinning with a Veltic or mackerel spinner does not really need an anti-kink device. On the other hand, in a big river like the Great Ouse, particularly if there is a strong flow on, you need both weight to get the bait down and an anti-kink device which actually works well. There is always a temptation to fish too light when spinning, but in heavy water conditions our advice is to make a bold decision, use plenty of weight, perhaps in the form of a half moon lead, and make sure the spinner is fishing deep and well. It soon becomes apparent if you have chosen too much weight, whereas the opposite isn't always obvious. Clearly, a combined weight-cum-anti-kink device is ideal. To sum up, if the line isn't becoming twisted (and to test for this simply drop the spinner on the ground to take out the line tautness) then keep spinning; if it does twist up add an anti-kink vane, preferably in the form of lead if you can.

These general remarks apply as much to fishing still waters from the bank as they do to rivers, particularly if the water is deep, and particularly with certain spinners which have a tendency to give kink trouble. At this point then, you will have your tackle assembled and be ready to cast. In a shallow lake with weed up to just below the surface it is often necessary to begin the retrieve immediately, attempting of course to work the bait into any pockets, and to choose spinners that come in slow and shallow, such as mackerel spinners, small Vibros, 1-inch minnows, Veltics and so on. In deeper water it is necessary to count the bait to the bottom on the first cast in order to ascertain relative depth. With many spinners you will know from experience just how many feet per second they sink, so your counting will give you the actual depth. On the next cast begin the retrieve at the depth you wish to fish.

There are two ways to conduct a count-down. One is to hold the lure on a tight line, in which case you are in direct contact the moment the retrieve begins; the second is to allow the spinner to sink under its own weight on a free line, in which case the retrieve causes the spinner to leave the bottom at a high angle before direct contact is made. Both methods are satisfactory as long as you realize what you are doing. When the bottom is snaggy the second method is probably better, for there is slightly less chance for the hooks to get caught up.

The actual retrieve has been debated for years, but as a generalisation or a starter at least, as slow and as deep a recover as possible is best.

Sometimes it is necessary to retrieve fast, and sometimes shallow, but begin with deep and slow. Personally we prefer a steady retrieve particularly when perch fishing, but there are times when working the rod top from side to side or up and down, or even fishing sink-and-draw, produces takes that the steady recovery didn't. The main trouble with a lively retrieve is that the fish may miss. Both pike and perch are bad shots in our view, and pike in particular may well rely almost entirely on vibrations rather than vision.

On most still waters it pays to try a cast or two along the bank, as well as a few casts standing well back from the bank. Because anglers may have baited up for roach it could be that pike and perch have moved in very close to the bank where the spinning man would normally stand. After fishing in this way, give the swim a fair old coverage, trying for depth and distance as well as areas marginal to weedbeds, if not *in* the weedbeds. We have always felt very strongly against the common advice to fish as round a clock face, each cast going a few degrees to one side of the last. It makes for boring and mechanical fishing. We much prefer to work out or guess where the fish might lie and then really concentrate on giving it to them. Once spinning becomes mechanical it is so easy to miss bites and lose lures, and the whole joy goes out of it even if neither of these probabilities materializes.

In river fishing the natural tendency is to fish across and downstream; and it is generally more common to use lead to get the bait down, and anti-kink vanes to avoid line twist. However, although most anglers seem to fish downstream it is neither necessary nor always desirable. When casting upstream there are several definite consequences. In the first place the lure comes back at you much more quickly, and although it obviously reaches the fish at the same speed (!) the fish actually has plenty of time to see the lure because as a rule it will be facing into the current. The angler also approaches his quarry from behind, and the main risk of frightening fish, given that the angler as usual avoids his shadow falling on the water, results from fish very close to the angler darting upstream and transmitting alarm ahead. When fishing downstream a frightened fish often darts away upstream going *away* from the fish you are after.

When fishing in Barmston Drain in the Hull city reaches, where there is considerable flow, Barrie found that pike fell much more readily to a spoon fished upstream than to one fished either downstream or across and down. In fact three times as many pike fell to the former method. We have found that the same obtains with other fish and on many other waters and would recommend that although upstream spinning is often hard work, needing twice as many casts, it should be given a real trial on small to medium rivers up to about the size of the middle reaches of the Great Ouse. With larger, deeper rivers upstream spinning may become just too difficult, but it is always worth a try to see what happens.

Across and downstream spinning should never become a mechanical process. Try to search out holes, give the lure a different line or different speed, and as in all fishing employ the craft as delicately and quietly as you can. We have sometimes had the feeling that footfalls on the riverside, as opposed to the lakeside, are less important: but still we fish quietly.

Avoidance of snags is always a problem, since the angler often tries to fish very close to them. This is understandable, as fish often shelter in the snags. One place where anglers commonly get fouled up is just before the spinner reaches the rod, at about the point where the river bottom (or, indeed, lake bottom) begins to slope upwards. Not only does debris collect here, but the angler often fails to raise his rod top gradually as the spinner nears home. Raising the rod top means that with a steady retrieve the spinner will continue parallel to and *above* the bottom contours, rather than ploughing into them close to the bank. A couple of casts is all that is needed to work out the best retrieve for the slope of the bank.

If you do get snagged up avoid savage pulling of any kind, but work your way downstream and try to tease the spinner gently off the obstruction. It is possible to float proprietary tackle-freers down the line, or even to convert a bottle for that purpose: these are attached to the line so that they are free sliding, and are then allowed to float well downstream of the spinner before being pulled again from the upstream end. It has the same effect, sometimes more efficiently, of walking downstream and pulling. You cannot use the same technique if you snag during upstream spinning, but you can walk upstream of the snag and pull from there.

There are many tricks to be learnt about spinning rivers, and new ones will come to the thinking angler. For example, it is sometimes possible to float a light spinner into position by placing it on a piece of wood and floating it downstream. If you are positioned on the inside of a bend it is occasionally possible to float your lure almost across and round the bend before retrieving, thus getting a longer retrieve than would have been possible by normal casting.

As with most spinning, we feel that the speed of retrieve should be steady rather than jerky, and the pace judged relative to the type of fish expected. Fred Wagstaffe once told us that in his opinion a big pike could and would overhaul any lure, whatever its speed, if it was attracted to it. On the other hand we're sure that you could outpace and outmanoeuvre a river perch, and perhaps a chub wouldn't deign to follow unless the spinner passed through his manor. Trout will sometimes chase spinners for enormous distances and it is probably impossible to outpace them.

Much of what we said in *Plugs and plug fishing* about boat fishing applies also to using spinners from boats on still waters, and we shall not duplicate much here. Basically there are two methods: either the boat is anchored and the spinners cast from it and retrieved, or else the spinner or spoon is trolled (trailed) behind. In the former case our remarks about bank fishing apply; in the latter some specialised techniques are an advantage. For example the boat rod rests shown in Photo. 39 help greatly in keeping the rod out of the boat but in reach of the fisherman. Without rests they have to be propped on the gunwhales on a bit of cloth to avoid damaging the rod. Takes when trolling are usually savage and the rod top whips round, and the fish usually hook themselves: here the main problem is stopping the progress of the boat before the rod or line snaps! Strong rods and lines are definitely more efficient, and frankly we would double up on all strengths for trailing spinners.

An alternative technique is to use a weight attached to the boat by a thin rope, and by a clip to the top of the trace, lowering the whole lot down to the desired fishing depth. The clip is designed to release the lure in the event of a take but the *line at the rod top goes slack*, at least momentarily, giving the angler a few seconds to think and act.

As a digression we would mention that some activities, now largely illegal in these islands, are still practised in the Soviet Union where the catch is invariably to be eaten. The rudder-like Otter Board is still used. Here the board works its way out at almost right-angles to the boat and then moves parallel to and maintains pace with the boat. Between the board and the boat are any number of spinners attached on short traces to the main line: a kind of highly mobile long lining. This method mostly succeeds with lake perch, trout and char, and is usually too shallowly fished for pike.

The same enterprising anglers use a similar system from the bank, either one man and his Otter Board, or two men (one on each bank) with a cord between them and numerous spinners. They either hold stationary position in a strong current, or walk along in a gentle one!

So far we haven't said anything about the anchored static (but spinning) spinner. This is a method used by salmon fishermen. A paternoster lead is attached by a link to a swivel some distance above the spinner. The tackle is cast into a swim of suitable depth and current, the lead takes a hold on the bottom, and the spinner streams out in the current: a kind of legered spinner! A deal of skill is needed not only in the actual fishing thereof, but in getting the right lead, and lure. Fished thus a pool can be very slowly covered. Surely here is an untried technique for pike rivers, although we have tried a vaguely similar method with plugs without much success.

Certain other matters will be dealt with in PART FOUR, where we deal with the catching of particular fish species, and at which point we hope for a crystallization of many matters.

39 Barrie's out-rigger for boat trolling.

10

Ultra-light spinning

Ultra-light spinning started two years ago for Ken on the River Towy, where he was early autumn fishing for sewin. Although the river was clearing after rain and seemed ideal in every respect for a fish or two, they had proved indifferent to the fly and the rod had been set aside until nightfall. Resting on a rock ledge above the Junction Pool Ken imagined he had the river to himself and was mildly surprised when another angler made his appearance on the opposite bank.

His rod looked very much like a cut-down split cane fly rod, to which was attached a small Altex fixed spool reel. The whole thing resembled a child's set-up and quite incapable of dealing with several pounds of fighting sewin — let alone the odd salmon that were also running. During the next fifteen minutes Ken witnessed some of the finest casting and spinning techniques that he has ever seen — either before or since. The small Mepps-type spinner seemed to twinkle in and out of every possible run and hold, resulting in a good fish taking where he (Ken) had been fishing unsuccessfully just a short time previously.

Any admiration that had been forthcoming for the spinning techniques was immediately eclipsed by the sheer skill displayed by the angler in playing that sewin, a four-pound fish that performed every trick in the calendar and one or two others besides. Although the line could not have been of greater breaking strain than two pounds, a break was avoided time after time by the angler who, when the moment of truth approached, merely altered the tension on the spool and gave the fish a nearly slack line. On the second time that this trick was used Ken realised he was watching a vintage performance — and suddenly also realised where he had seen the style described. It was straight from the pages of an Alexander Wanless book.

On his return from holiday Ken contacted Ron Coleby, the antique book seller near Lincoln, and thanks to his industry and interest managed to assemble a complete set of all the Wanless works. The words of that firey and pugnacious writer proved so challenging that it was immediately decided to emulate his 1920 style, and spin with ultra-light tackle.

Vic Gibson, the rod maker at Dons of Edmonton's tackle shop, was enlisted to help find a modern equivalent of a Wanless wand. After days spent in discussion and many more in experimenting with various blanks, a Fibatube 7-foot No. 4 fly rod was selected which had 3 inches lopped from its tip, stiffening its action slightly.

In keeping with the Wanless tradition the solid cork handle, 15 inches long, was smoothed parallel, leaving a dome at either end to stop the lightweight plastic Fuji reel fittings from sliding off. Rod rings presented a problem: Fuji rings were used for the end ring and for a single leg butt ring. But it was not possible to match any of the stand-off types of proprietary ring to fit as intermediates. Eventually Vic, with great patience, manufactured some himself from 28 gauge steel wire.

40 Perch taken on the ultra-light outfit.

Whipping them into place was another patient task, as they had to be tied on the sides of the blank instead of mounting flat with the normal foot fittings.

Finding a matching reel was another problem only solved when John Hennes, the Shakespeare rep., suggested his company's closed face match reel. Quite apart from a fast retrieve, the reel had big advantages in allowing a fish to be played from the handle, together with an adjustable drag situated on the side plate of the body — easily accessible should one suddenly want to let a fish run, à la Wanless. Matched with 2-lb breaking strain Sylcast line, the whole outfit proved light as a feather, accurate as a rifle and, more important still, as resilient as a spring.

The beauty of a new type of rod is that it inspires one to try new techniques and methods. We (yes, Barrie liked the set-up and equipped himself with a similar outfit) soon found ourselves looking at a whole range of lightweight lures that we had previously decided to be too small for practical casting with our standard spinning rods.

As our new ultra-light so closely resembled a fly rod it was natural that our imagination should first turn to spinning reservoir lures. We had,

41 1. Red-throat tube minnow. 2. The 'bent' polystickle. 3. Cohoki plug/spoon. 4. Mackerel spinner.

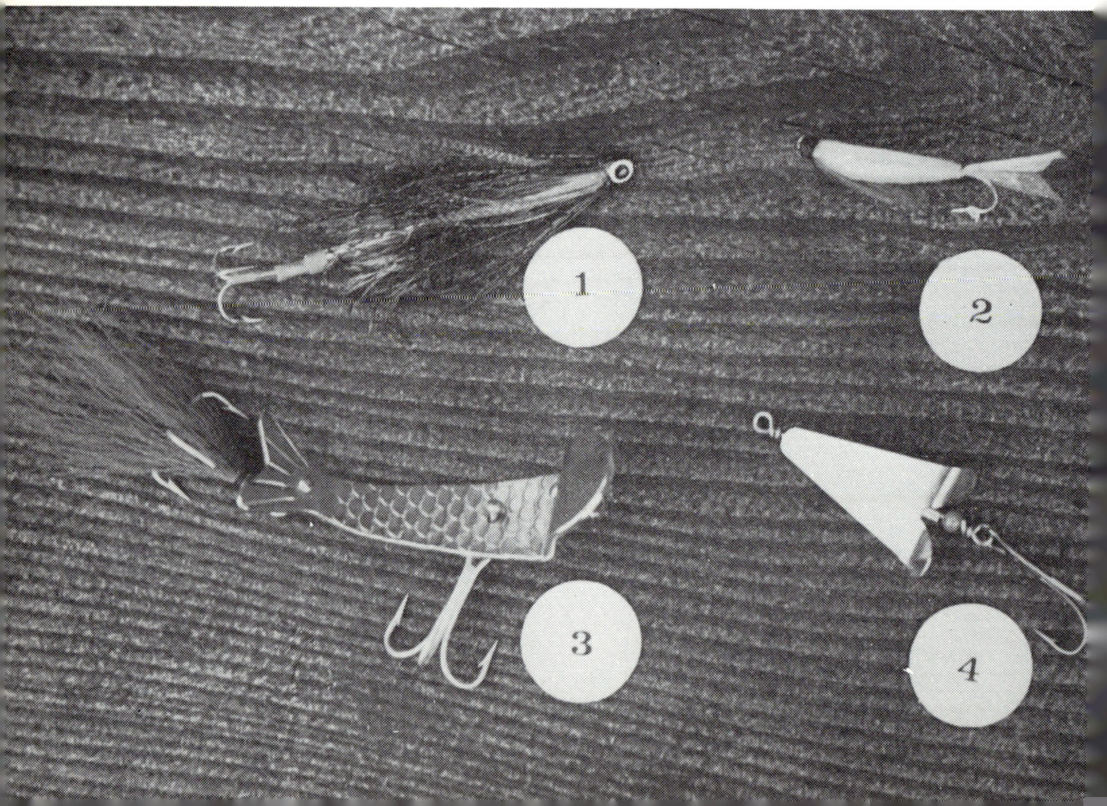

for a long time, been using Muddler Minnows and Polystickles as a lure with a small fold-over lead, or swan shot pinched a foot or so above the hook to help achieve distance with a cast. Then, browsing through a 1920 Hardy Catalogue we spotted a coloured photo of salmon flies with spinning vanes mounted in front of the head.

A talk with Dennis Howell, the pro fly tier at Dons, resulted in the production of a large imitation roach, with weighted body and spinning vane at the head (Photo. 17(1) on page 55). We also prevailed on him to produce some tube flies tied as minnows (Photo. 41(1)) and his imitation of a red-throat shown in that illustration turned out to be so life-like that we have asked him to experiment further with an identical model complete with spinning vanes, or a small bar spinner at the head.

The Polystickle has long been a tried favourite, as we mentioned earlier. But we fancied one that would have a definite wobble, as opposed to the normal straight retrieve. Dennis managed to find (?) some large bent-shank hooks and somehow tied a lure to these. The result, retrieved with a swan shot pinched a short way up the line, is a beautiful swooping wobble that has taken for us — as indeed have all flies we have described — some excellent chub (see Photo. 41(2)).

Still in the fly category, we have now accumulated a fair selection of fly-spoons in different sizes and, of course, the Mepps fly spinners with an imitation Palmer tied on the long-shanked treble. Wooden and small metal Devon minnows, quill minnows (alas, no longer made from quill) and the new soft plastic minnows with nose-mounted bar spinners by Abu or Mepps are all musts in our tackle boxes.

But best of all with this little wand is the natural bait, the preserved minnows that are single treble mounted, and small sprats mounted on leaded spinning rigs. We have both discussed the success obtained by using the ultra-light in this way, and have arrived at the conclusion that one reason is probably because we are fishing with a completely home-made outfit — rod- and lure-wise at least — which gives one the confidence needed to really work for a fish.

Mind you, playing a fish to the bank, a good fish that is, can be no small achievement. As is so often the case one sets off to catch one species of fish and finishes up with another that is totally unsuited to the tackle you are using. This perversity on the part of fish is such that some of Ken's most exciting pike days have occurred with the ultra-light when he was really after perch or chub.

If you hit a good fish in running water then all that Wanless ever wrote on free-lining a fish into submission usually works, and works well. The moment a hard run is commenced then the tension is practically removed from the spool on the reel, and the fish allowed its wilful way with only a gentle reminder that there is a restriction. Wanless maintained that this gentle pressure was better than all the bullying in the world, and that it worried a fish into exhausting itself in half the time it took with heavy gear and brute force.

But what about the fish hooked in still water? Give him free line and he will merely cruise off somewhere and sulk on the bottom — usually at

42 The ultra-light rod in action.

some distance from the angler, and with so much line out that no amount of heaving will make the slightest impression.

Well, the cure for that situation can be obtained by looking at Photo. 42. From it you can see just how much spring there is in the little rod, and provided that the rod tip is kept as near to vertical as is possible, then that spring will keep sudden and direct strain off the line and prevent a break in the majority of cases. Of course, there comes the moment of truth in this situation as in any other, when a fish just keeps going despite all the line pressure you dare give, and though the rod be bent nearly double. But that is a great part of the pleasure in angling, and if a break should occur, then reason with yourself that had it not been for the lightweight approach, then possibly the fish would not have been hooked in the first place.

Actually, that last statement sums up our whole approach to the ultra-light outfit. We use it when normally the conditions of weather or water would never let us consider spinning with any of our normal methods or when smallish fish are to be expected. Therefore we find we enjoy a few extra days spinning during the season with the minimum of discomfort from portly or cumbersome tackle. Just a little rod, a reel, and two small boxes of tiny lures or mounted minnows can provide a staggering day's sport.

PART FOUR
Spinning for coarse fish

11

Spinning for pike

This is the sport of which boyhood dreams are made, and one of the few branches of the sport which caters for that perennial problem of all youngsters, namely their inability to sit still for more than five minutes at a time. Spinning is essentially a mobile sport and like all mobile pike-fishing methods it teaches you a great deal about the species, its habits, its speed off the mark and power, its measure of accuracy; and all this because you so often *see* the fish, sometimes at your feet where it materializes out of nothing, occasionally charging across the top of weedbeds having spotted your twinkling lure from up to twenty yards away, and sometimes with spectacular aerobatics as it strikes in shallow water. Barrie spent hundreds of hours as a youngster spinning for pike in the shallow railway pits and clay workings around Eastrington in East Yorkshire, and has seen as many as five hungry jacks chasing one mackerel spinner. To a youngster in those days spinning meant just that, because plugs were expensive and spinners were easier to make anyway. Mackerel spinners were used by Barrie because they were cheap, could be cast a long way on 8 lb b.s. line, and they really catch pike. The best he ever saw, taken by an acquaintance out at the same game, was 25 lb, although several double-figure fish fell prey to the same lure over a period of two or three years. Sometimes, where a 'hole' went down to 3-5 feet a small Colorado was used, with the red wool tag removed: somehow, on these tiny intimate waters, a red wool tail (equivalent to the bucktail of many North American lures) seemed just too conspicuous. A better substitute was a piece of Rhode Island Red chicken feather tied to the treble hook in the form of a roach's tail: this certainly encouraged that bonus fish, the perch, to take hold — and pike too, when they were tending to follow the lure and snip at the end without firmly taking.

As an aside, we could mention that this 'coming short' problem has been solved in another way by some of today's anglers, in the creation of the Commando spoons. In this case a flying treble follows the main spoon treble; a technique also used by salmon anglers. No doubt the flying treble is often taken by the pike, but more often it is foul hooked by it when striking the spoon blade itself. The technique is highly effective, but has been roundly condemned by many anglers, including some of the leading writers. We never use this method, a matter of personal choice, but find it difficult ultimately to condemn it as unsporting. Clearly it is a matter for the individual to decide.

But returning to those shallow Eastrington railway ponds and the lessons learned. Probably the first thing was to appreciate that additions to the line in the form of traces, anti-kink vanes and weights was something to be borne with fortitude when necessary. Traces are absolutely vital for pike spinning. Barrie once had twenty-seven pike in succession without a trace, average weight about 2 lb each, then hooked three doubles in a row on Carlton Towers, and lost them all! The bigger the mouth, the easier it is to engulf a spinner. On one occasion a 7-inch spoon completely disappeared into the back of the throat of a 17-pounder that Barrie had in Ireland. So if anybody tells you that traces are not necessary, make a booking for him in the local institution. He won't be lonely, for such places must be heavily populated by frustrated anglers.

On these small pits it is also strikingly obvious that spinning traces should be as thin a wire as possible and dark in colour, preferably black or sorrel-coloured, and never thick, plastic-coated and shiny. Shiny swivels and link swivels, not to mention anti-kink vanes, probably attract pike, but shiny traces do not. Barrie has a very clear memory of fishing a dull Veltic on a shiny, plastic-coated trace, and from thirty yards away could see the trace, but not the lure, as it made its way to his vantage point part-way up a railway embankment. So use a thin, dark trace, say 10-15 lb b.s. for most spinning; about a foot or 18 inches long, with a safety-pin link swivel at the business end, and a small bronze swivel at the other for attachment to the reel line. Personally, we feel that the reel line should *not* be tied direct to a loop in the trace wire, a method advocated by Richard Walker for attaching bait rigs, since the wire is so much finer than that of a swivel eye and *must* have a greater tendency to cut, cheese-wire fashion, the softer nylon line.

If weight cannot be added to the body of the spinner we add it, when necessary, to the line just above the trace rather than to the trace itself. It is much more convenient when changing lures or methods to remove the lead weight or weights from the line and then discard the bottom 6 inches of line and tie a new knot. Anti-kink vanes can be fixed in the same position, or a combination of the two in some instances. We think you have the attitude about right if you need your arm twisting to add anything other than a trace to your terminal tackle.

The main technique on those tiny waters, and one which has certainly worked all over Britain since then, was to spin over, under and around weed beds and snags, and along the bankside under overhanging trees. Line was usually 7 or 8 lb b.s. monofil, and despite the inferior monofil of the 1950's only certain spinners introduced 'spontaneous coiling' in the line. Colorados, minnows, and mackerel spinners, the three favourites, had little adverse effect and it was possible to wander from swim to swim flicking the tackle lightly under bushes and through small gaps in the floating or lightly-rooted reed mace beds. Little home-made minnows with reversible fins could always take out the kinks, or the line could be laid out in a field and trailed behind the angler for a few minutes.

Rods, in those carefree days, were a joke. Not that good rods weren't available, but under the age of twenty-one it wasn't possible to take out a mortgage. So we used sawn-off roach rods, parts of steel tank aerial and so on. Indeed, the rod is not really so important, nice though it is to have a wand of beautiful action. When Barrie went back there on a flying visit, much later, he took only the reel, some sellotape, and a safety pin: the rod was cut from a hedge, the pin and reel bound to the 'rod' and three pike from $1\frac{1}{2}$ lb to 4 lb were caught in three hours. Distance wasn't the object, in fact it would put you into the middle of a cornfield, but the real skill was from the split second the spinner hit the water to the split second of lifting it from the water.

Length of rod is certainly important. We went through the whole gamut of 4-foot to 11-foot with every half foot in between, and even on small waters of the type just described a rod of about 9-10 feet is ideal. It can be fished in almost all tight corners, admittedly reverting to underhand swings and catapult casts sometimes: remember, too, that in such circumstances distance casting is not necessary. Although a short rod will fire the spinner in a straight and accurate line to the target, with a long rod you can lob and loop the spinner with accuracy since the *slower* trajectory gives you time to correct. When distance *is* required then the longer rod again wins, this time hands down. Another consideration is the length of retrieve. Using a short rod the spinner is drawn back right to your feet — the most fish-scaring position, whereas the tip of a long rod can be held several feet down the bank and the spinner retrieved to that point. On small waters, as long a retrieve as possible gives a slow striker just that little bit more time to catch the spinner.

You can, of course, stick a 10-foot rod through the foliage and 'dap', much after the fashion of chub fishing. When Barrie was a youngster jigs were not readily available, but he took a number of pike by jigging a spinner in just such circumstances, even amongst thick *Potamogeton* beds. The trouble was that although the spinner *attracted* the pike easily enough to within inches of the bait, they came short much more commonly than with conventionally pulled spinners. It was found that a fly or a large lure with tied on jay feathers, or a small fly-spoon succeeded much better. Some of today's jigs would be better still. Nevertheless this technique did produce enough fish and certainly meant you could fish in places which other anglers walked past.

This kind of piking, producing small pike with the occasional double, is to be recommended for many of the reasons given, but perhaps above all for the way in which it forces you to cast in any and all directions, and with any and all obstructions, whether above the water or below it. It also teaches you to *plan* the landing of a fish in advance: every swim you approach needs looking at from two standpoints, firstly, where to lay the net down to draw the fish over; secondly, where to strike so that half a hawthorn bush isn't included in the pantomime. Talking of snags, one pike took a spinner, one treble point of which was buried in a thin springy underwater branch, the strike being so savage that it pulled the spinner free and hooked the pike, a 2 lb fish, simultaneously. The variety of interest, observation, and spectacle in such fishing is quite unending.

On the big waters piking takes on a new dimension, with a proportionate increase of the chance of some boring spinning. Don't misunderstand us here, for most of our spinning has been done on big waters; rivers, drains, lakes, loughs and lochs. And there is always the chance of a really giant pike to fire the imagination and keep the spinners and spoons working busily away! But faced with a lot of water, where on earth and how on earth does one make a start? Certainly, what you do *not* do is to start at point A, cast systematically 'round the clock face', move on to point B, perhaps ten yards down the bank, and do the same again. This is what makes big waters boring. After an hour or so, unless you've taken a fish or two, you begin to wonder why on earth you came. Remember that the fishing itself has to be enjoyable, not just the

43 Small spinners produced these pike within an hour when Ken fished a Lea valley pit.

catching of fish. The 'clock face' approach is fundamentally wrong, and when you think about it logically the idea could be taken to ridiculous extremes. For example, having worked through a swim at 5° angles with one spinner, why not try the next spinner, and the next, and the next . . . You'd spend all day in one swim. So even this so-called systematic approach isn't really systematic at all.

By all means search a swim carefully before moving on, but try to do it thinkingly, working out where the pike lie, and what spinner is likely to be best under the circumstances. When moving on, your objective should be the next swim you think may hold a pike or two, *not* the next one down the bank.

It is true that a systematic approach sometimes pays dividends. Two instances come to mind. The first concerned some friends, spinner/spoon men only, who used systematically to fish the lower Great Ouse and the Relief Channel: each swim was given one or two casts with a biggish Toby which was fired to the far bank and then retrieved close to the bottom. They reckoned that a couple of casts showed the spoon to any pike that was interested and then they moved on, leap-frogging each other, looking for big, actively feeding pike. A second concerned fishing on the Market Weighton canal where Barrie used to make a cast to the far bank, at right-angles to the flow; retrieve, and then take one step and cast again. The idea was that the small Copper and Silver (with red inside) would be certain to pass by a sizeable pike at least every few casts and it could not avoid seeing the spoon. This worked very well and he caught plenty of pike averaging 3-4 lb. His companion at the time was Phil Reeves, who worked ahead of Barrie, casting as his fancy took him. It was noticeable that Barrie took more pike.

44 Barrie setting out for a day's spinning.

Even on that water, however, the better fish, over ten pounds, fell to Veltic spinners worked through junction pools, at points where ditches and dykes entered the canal, and in some of the shelving holes between sandbars and weed beds. The same techniques worked well on the Yorkshire Derwent, which is a pretty sizeable river in places: find a feature such as the sunken barges at Sutton, and you have located pike more quickly.

Returning to the subject of large lochs and loughs, the standard technique is trolling (colloquial) or trailing (supposedly correct terminology), but whether this or any other method is used the idea is to break down the loch, mentally, into a series of smaller waters. Not only is this psychologically better, but it has a basis in pike ecology, for the species is not evenly distributed throughout a water. Find yourself a bay, perhaps a hundred yards or more across, a stream entering in the corner, shallows with soft weeds and fringing emergent reeds, a drop off to 25-feet plus at the mouth of the bay, and you have found a potential pike-holding area, perhaps even a hotspot. You can fish such a bay quietly by anchoring and spinning round the boat, the technique which Ray Webb, Fred Wagstaffe and others found so successful in Eire. A variety of spinners can be tried, and then the boat can be up-anchored and a different part of the bay tried. These are the circumstances where we would normally use sizeable spoons; Tobys, Pikers, and homemade monstrosities of various lengths and colours. Generally speaking, such large waters are crystal clear and the tone of the spoon is important. Almost all spinning enthusiasts in recent years have confirmed the old adage of a bright spoon for dull conditions and a dull one for bright conditions, and we agree wholeheartedly with this. The thinking behind what has been proved in practice is that in sunny, clear conditions a bright spoon is too open to inspection by the pike just before it strikes. Our experiments in the flume tank suggest another reason. Bearing in mind that the pike homes in to a considerable extent on vibration (its eyes must lose sight of the lure just before impact) and that it is not all that accurate a shot, it may be that the extra flash under sunlight actually puts off the pike by making it doubt its own accuracy. The vibrations would be the same but the pike's vision might be seriously affected by the very irregular, strong flashes from some spoons and, in fact, they may see the spinner or spoon less well. But whatever the reason, dull spoons for bright conditions is a good adage.

Casting from an anchored boat should be done standing up. Whilst this might seem to strike at rules for safety, the real safety-first tricks are

45 Spinning from the standing position.

to use a proper boat for the job, be shipshape, wear a life jacket, and fish with a companion. Sitting down and casting is highly inefficient, and the only time we contemplate it is if a pike follows the spoon to the boat: then we sit down very slowly before casting again.

Have the landing net hanging on the thole pin or rowlocks, so that it is not in the way. It should have a short handle, or you can use a large triangular net without a handle. Hold the frame open with both hands (if you are the netsman, of course) and close it when the fish is enmeshed, then lift out the net by grasping the mesh. We often leave the netted pike in the water for a few moments whilst we tidy up the boat preparatory to unhooking.

Trolling is often condemned as boring, but probably becomes so only to people not fishing properly. The same rules about finding the pike apply: *never* troll on mile after mile in an unthinking fashion. Try the bays, the contours, changes of depth, changes of lures and so on. In fact, trolling is a skilled business whether one has the rods more or less inboard, pointing over the gunwhales, or has them on outriggers (Photo. 39 on page 93). The line for trolling big lochs for big pike probably needs to be in the 18 to 25 lb b.s. bracket, not because that is needed to land the fish, but because in the event of a take (with the anti-reverse lever *on*, of course) the pike hooks itself and the boat's forward movement must be stopped pronto otherwise a snapped line will result. If the anti-reverse lever is off, or the clutch set light, the pike will not necessarily hook itself, and by the time the rod is picked up, in say 3-5 seconds, the fish has thrown the lure.

Both trolling and spinning from a stationary boat are techniques that can be continued with natural bait fishing at lunchtimes! Simply hook a few sprats on the trebles and chuck it out to lay on the bottom. Barrie had an 8 lb fish on the R. Hull like this, and on two occasions has had a pike pick up a static spinner on the bottom, the first a sizeable fish on the R. Hull which picked up a Veltic but eventually got off, and the second a 4 lb fish on L. Ree which picked up a Colorado and didn't get off.

Lunchtime on a big loch is also a useful time for breaking with these traditional methods and trying something a little different. What we often do is look for an extensive area of rocky, reedy shallows or flooded fields, and drift quietly into them looking for basking pike which are then approached from either the boat or the bank depending upon which is most convenient. This is an essentially good way to relax after lunch, and after a full morning on the open water, but does not necessarily mean small pike only: on one occasion a friend took one of 27 lb. It is also a good way of getting to know a loch before facing up to venturing forth on the open water. Barrie can remember on many occasions catching several pike at lunchtime, spinning the shallows, and collecting nothing at all during the rest of the day!

On Loch Lomond on one occasion, the pike had obviously moved into some flooded fields, and strikes could be seen amongst emergent lesser bulrush clumps and the long grass. On closer investigation we found that the pike were feeding on toads which had gathered for spawning. Most of the time these toads were sitting on the bottom, in the grass, and safely out of sight. But the moment one came up for air a V-shaped wake was seen coming at it like a torpedo, often from ten or more yards away: the pike were clearly watching and waiting. Under these circumstances one would have thought that a plug would succeed with the pike, but they failed, including a floating rubber frog, yet spinners succeeded in taking three! It is, of course, quite easy to fish in emergent grass since

46 Just hooked! Large trebles need driving well home if they are to stay.

most of the stems are firm yet flexible so that the treble hooks slide through them quite easily. It is a situation that calls for a return to the earlier methods of this chapter, namely small shallow water spinners, although if the surface of the water is really rough a big Piker spoon worked very shallow, even from wave to wave, can be highly effective. Even quite small pike will chase a big spoon in a swim of this nature.

The kind of pike spinning we have been talking about is clearly very variable, and you must learn to cast and fish the lures in a manner of ways, ranging from the trolled downrigger to the flicked 1-inch minnow on 7 lb b.s. line. But there is a casting stance that we like to adopt, given that the situation is not too cramped. We face the water, standing, except on those Fenland drains like the Old Bedford which have quaking margins and need a very quiet, creeping approach. The cast is usually double-handed over the right shoulder, the rod coming through at an angle of about 60° to the ground. All these factors vary with the circumstances, of course, but less variable is the retrieve position. Here it is necessary to point the rod nearly at the lure, at an angle of perhaps 25° as seen in plan view. If you point directly at the lure there is a slight risk of snapping on the take. If the rod is at right-angles to the retrieve line of the spinner, as it sometimes has to be, then it may be difficult to get in a full-blooded strike to drive home the hooks.

The actual take of a pike varies tremendously from the savage thump as it hits the spinner crossways, or snaps it up from behind, in both cases often stopping its rush in an instant, to the almost perch-like pluck as it cruises after the lure snipping at the tail treble. If a pike comes up really fast from behind, which often happens in rivers, a slack line bite may ensue as the pike actually continues its headlong rush. Not only is the spinner often completely engulfed by this kind of attack, but the angler must give a really sweeping strike to take up the slack. Fortunately, with an engulfed spinner there is little chance of missing. Probably the worst thing that can happen is a pike following the spinner right to the bank edge. With a floating plug or wobbled deadbait you can stop the retrieve, allowing the plug to float and the deadbait to sink, but with a spinner or spoon you have to keep on reeling. Some advise speeding-up the retrieve, but we try to continue it, while making it clear to the pike by raising the spinner's route to the surface that very shortly the lure will reach the bank. If the pike still refuses, and you are able to creep away without frightening it off, try another cast from about ten yards along the bank, casting back to where the pike is lying. You can also change to to a small spinner at the same time. When spinning fish baits, as on Archer flights or home-made versions, the strike of the pike is treated in the same way as when using a spinner or spoon, but when wobbling deadbaits, even small ones like sprats, it is as well to ease off in the event of a take and treat it much as you would a dead or livebait run. This takes a great deal of will-power for us, but luckily the take on a wobbled deadbait is often gentle. The savage takes to sprats *can* be struck immediately, but we usually miss most of them if we do this, probably as a result of the soft sprat balling up and masking the hooks.

So far we have outlined the spinners and spoons and the natural bait approach, but there is a combination of the two which may well be one of the methods of the future. We refer to the baited spoon technique. This has been used extensively in sea fishing and North American 'sportfishing', found to be effective in perch fishing and, in our chapter on that subject, we refer to our feeling that this species homes in on a scent trail through the water. The diagram (Fig. H) is of a rig considered by some to be very effective for pike, and it must be admitted that here is a potential method of pike fishing that might work well on waters where the pike are sick of the sight of spinners and wobbled deadbaits. In ancient days the baited spinner or spoon was certainly used much more than today, and just as night fishing for pike needed a few pioneers in the later 1960s, this technique really needs trying. It would surely be wrong to say that a wobbled deadbait can achieve anything a baited spoon can, because the flashing spoon acts as an attractor, and the bait itself can be quite small on occasions to encourage the pike which come short. As far as the natural bait is concerned certainly strips of mackerel or trout, or chunks of freshly killed roach would have an undoubted attraction.

When it comes to considering baits for wobbling techniques the choice is legion. Sprats last about half an hour if frozen to start with, but mounting up a new sprat is such a quick and easy business — we often merely put the sliding treble of a snap tackle through the snout and tie it firmly in position — and sprats are so small and light, that it hardly matters if you have to change baits every fifteen minutes. Whole herrings and mackerel soon get pretty scraggy but may be no less effective for that, except that they don't cast too well. But a good solid roach in the 5-8 oz bracket is the most convenient, and perhaps the most killing bait. Jim Gibbinson's idea (1974) of slitting the belly of the bait to remove the insides, not only allows the wobbled bait to sink very slowly indeed, but actually seems to give a longer period before the bait breaks up. The only time we've had trouble with such baits disintegrating is when they really do a belly flop at the end of a long cast. There really can be no doubt that the smell of a freshly killed roach is attractive to pike. A bait that is firm at the beginning of the day can sometimes be used all day unless the pike chew it to pieces, and in that case no one would complain.

In our chapter on spinning natural baits we refer to our favourite technique of preserving them, failing a deep-freeze that is. At one time we were not too worried about formalin-soaked baits, but more recently have come around to using sugar solution at a stage immediately following the formalin soak. While it would be much better to con your supplier into putting a few roach into his deep freeze, it is worth remembering that the freezer compartment of an ordinary household fridge will keep baits fresh for several weeks at least. In the winter months a bag full of deadbaits will stay solidly frozen all day, but in summer it is better to attempt to calculate more or less the number needed for the day, because frozen baits soon thaw. Preserved baits are probably better in the warmer months, but at this time of the year it is much easier to get freshly killed baits.

Wobbled deadbait fishing, or deadbait spinning as it is often called (slightly erroneously), can be carried out extremely slowly. In fact there is a gradual transition as follows: static deadbait; twitched deadbait; wobbled deadbait; spun deadbait. The first of these usually has the head end of the deadbait hanging downwards, whereas all the more mobile methods have the bait head upwards along the trace. In order to be thoroughly flexible in approach on the day it is quite possible to fish static deadbaits head upwards too.

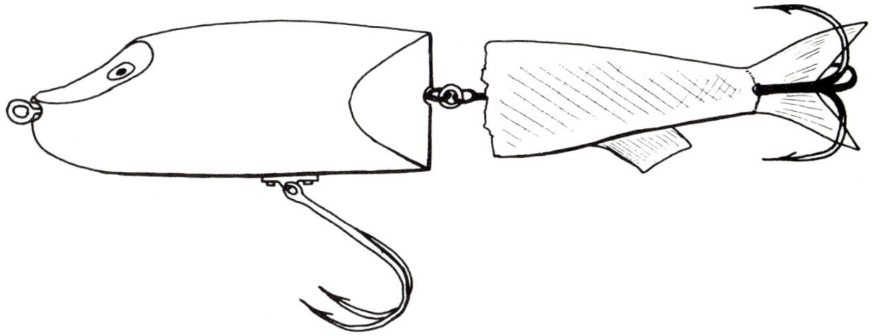

Fig. **H**

Wobbling deadbaits in really deep water is not easy, but from a boat it is possible to drift along bumping them and twitching them along the bottom, a technique found to work well on Irish loughs. This particular method is transitional to trolled deadbaits, where the usual role of the spoon is played by a slowly drawn deadbait mounted in exactly the same way as for wobbled deadbaiting from the bank. In really shallow water rough conditions seem to be best for chucking out deadbaits, but we are uncertain whether our observations are really objective on this issue. We shouldn't be at all surprised to hear of anglers succeeding well in calm water conditions. Jim Gibbinson has succeeded well with a smallish deadbait allowed to float on calm water and twitched gently at intervals. As a matter of fact we haven't yet had a fish like this but have seen several pike take a small dead roach just after we've thrown it back in! The deadbait can be retrieved from wave to wave, but not with the same speed as a big Jim Vincent style spoon. Takes are usually pretty savage to both lures, but on the deadbait it is fairly common to get a crafty grab in which the pike takes the bait and then simply sinks out of sight, often creating slack line.

It must be clear from the foregoing that the use of spinners, spoons, spun baits and wobbled baits for pike is a very variable art. This does not mean that it is necessary for you to carry a huge load. In fact the only (necessary) nuisance item is a large landing net. Spoons etc. can be carried in boxes in the pockets of a good waistcoat or Bob Church jacket, and we prefer rucksacks on our backs (rather than shoulder bags), using these to carry our food and small items of gear — camera, waterproof trousers, drink and so on. If you must do a *lot* of spinning in winter, follow our advice in chapter 4 about keeping warm. Taking weed from the hooks is the worst thing about winter spinning, though gloves with the fingers removed help a lot with the hands. Waders we always consider valuable, not only for wading, but for keeping the legs warm. In fact the only improvement we can suggest as far as both go is to well-vaseline your toes before putting on an old pair of socks to go into bootees and sea boot socks. Equipped in this way the angler should be both mobile and warm for winter pike spinning.

12

Spinning for perch and chub

PERCH

We wrote the perch section of *Plugs and plug fishing* with a deep lament at the passing of that fine species, and even went so far as to suggest that the pages in that chapter should be black-edged to mourn such a great passing. Now, just over two years or so later, we find a rather different picture with perch creeping back into the news — and good fish too, weighing pounds in the plural and from a cross-section of waters as widely divergent as industrial stretches of the River Lea, gravel pits and private lakes and, best of all, reports indicating sizeable fish again appearing in some of the big reservoirs.

We suggest that there is probably a good head of perch in some waters today, but that they are not being chased by the specialist angler, if ever they really were before the mysterious disease and demise occurred a few years back. In fact, we would even suggest that, prior to the disease, perch were never desperately sought after and mostly were caught accidentally.

Fortunately for us, the authors of old angling books excelled in telling anglers where fish could be found, something writers of today rarely bother to do. So hearsay and legend tell us that the place to look for perch is along camp sheathing, around bridges, high banks, locks and weirs. Anywhere, in fact, that man has had a hand in re-styling that which nature usually does to perfection.

What many writers failed to give were the reasons *why* you should look for perch in those locations: the simple fact that this is where small fry can congregate in reasonable safety, and where natural food in the form of insects will wash and accumulate to form a natural hunting ground for predatory fish like the perch. Moral? To find good perch, think like one that is looking for a meal, and you will usually score. Find one perch and it is odds-on that you will find a shoal, probably evenly graded in size and stupid enough in the smaller sizes to let you catch fish after fish from the same place, always providing that you do not become careless and prick or lose one. Even the lowest I.Q. has its break factor, and a prick from an angler's hook happens to be the one possessed by a perch.

We have been perch spinning for enough years now to have learned where not to look for them, and when not to fish. We avoid very fast water; that hump of flesh on the shoulders of a perch would disappear at a rapid rate with exercise. We leave mud bottoms on river or lake beds well alone, our experience telling us that perch may well be there 'hoovering' the bottom for food, but if they are, they are not likely to be very interested in a spinner of any sort. Flood water, or water that is coloured in any way can also take the edge off a day's fishing. Whether it is the suspended grit and mud content that puts them off feed, or just the fact that their eyesight is poor, is anyone's guess.

Weather plays an enormous part in perch feeding patterns. Excessive rain, as we have pointed out, can put them off feed, and cold, real biting

47 Seeking perch among moored boats.

cold, will also put them off but on a diminishing scale. The longer the cold lasts and the lower the temperature drops, so interest in food falls. Not only that, but cold also drives them into deeper water and down to the bottom until eventually they become nearly as torpid as tench. Natural baits score better at these times.

The most influential factor affecting feeding is the degree of brightness in the weather. On bright, sunny days perch will be close to the surface, working into the shallows and interested only in playing at feeding, although everything that comes before them will be well investigated. Warm, dull days when there is plenty of light behind a cloud base but no direct sunlight are just about the best for spinning and a good shoal will feed hard, barely questioning anything that is spun before them. By far the best day for a big fish has for us been one of those back end, late February, early March days when a gradual warm-up has given just a hint of spring. A little weak sunshine and we have both hit good perch when we have been pike spinning and using large baits that we would never, by choice, have considered for a perch.

There is a school of thought that brackets pike and perch together, maintaining that what is good for one must hold good for the other, be it rod, strength of line or size of lure. Nothing could be further from the truth. We have described the odd day when a perch will conform to the principles of pike feeding, but those occasions are few and far between. For all their schoolboy, first fish, big-mouthed, hungry image they are as delicate at feeding as a roach, at least where sizeable fish are concerned, and deserve as much consideration as that species in deciding on tackle and tactics.

Our chapter on tackle selection decreed that size of lure should govern the line, rod and reel. We work to a bait weight of approximately 10 grams as the maximum we wish to use for perch fishing, and consider that this supports a line with no greater breaking strain than 4 lb and a rod 6- to 7-feet long with matching reel. Of course, this size of outfit tends to minimise the distance one can cast, but serious perch fishing is not a long and repeated series of massive casts into the very middle of a water where one happens to be fishing. Imagination is the thing that catches perch; imagining where small fry are likely to be, and that is rarely going to be miles away from the bankside.

Instead of worrying about distance we think of ways to reach obvious perch holds without disturbing them or being seen — a thought often omitted by the spinning angler. A cast of fifteen feet made with the angler standing in a concealed position is more likely to achieve success

48 Fresh woods and pastures new. Vic Gibson making good use of breast-high waders.

than one of fifty feet made with the angler standing above the skyline, and after ten minutes of bank-stamping and bush-whacking to get into position. Where it is not possible to get near to a good casting position by using the bank, one can often reach it by using the water, providing that it is safe. Vic Gibson sold us on that idea — he invested in a set of breast-high waders and found that with a little care he could reach areas on some of his local gravel pits where no-one had ever spun before (see Photo. 48). Not only that, his position low down in the water gave him the obvious advantage of keeping out of sight of the fish.

Obviously, weather must govern the type of lure that you spin with. A warm, sunny day and fish in the shallows demand the smallest bait possible — and this for us is a tiny copper fly-spoon with perhaps one small shot to help in making the cast unless, of course, we are using the ultra-light rod and closed face reel. The tiny Shakespeare Dorado bar spinner is another excellent worker, and available in a variety of colours that allow ringing the changes until the right one is found. Whether colour on a revolving blade has any influence or not (and we are still in some doubt after our tank tests) the black and yellow model has been our most successful.

No matter how attractive a lure may be, it can prove useless when it is worked inconsistently or thoughtlessly. For fishing an area where perch are known to lie, a direct cast right over them followed by a retrieve through the shoal will lead to disaster. Line falling across the surface in good visibility can literally be seen in a flash. Far better is a cast made to one side or other of the shoal and a steady retrieve with the hope of enticing a fish out to take it.

One can get away with casting beyond and retrieving over fish in rough water conditions such as those around a weirpool, and of course you can scale-up the lure size considerably. Several spoons are absolutely great for this type of work, notable the Paravan type of Norwegian spoon, beautifully finished and producing a firm, half-wobbled part-spin that really pulls them in. Other spoons in this category are the Shakespeare Jim Vincent and Catcher, and the Abu Flamingo. As far as is possible we plump for near-perch colours or, failing that, a part red and gold finish.

One lure has been especially useful to us when fishing weirpools and lock areas during the autumn months. At this time large shoals of small (and often not so small) fish are up against timbers and supports, feeding on silkweed, which is just beginning to die off and flake away. The little Mepps Adour worked around these places seems to beat the ordinary bar spinners at this time. It looks like a small fish, but even better, responds to a sink and draw retrieve that pulls perch when a straightforward wind leaves them cold. The woollen tassel on the tail is an optional extra — we have taken our fish both with and without it. The only disadvantage of wool around any hook is that it tends to encourage rusting.

Weirpool fishing can be a labour of love at times. The best time to spin is when the water level is low and there is plenty of slack water either side of the main run and around the closed gates. Directly there is a hard pull of water one's chances disappear. But the attraction of a weir with its 'fishy' atmosphere can often lead one to waste hours of unproductive fishing.

Stillwaters and large open stretches of river where there is a reasonable depth are the places where we spin with larger baits, such as the Toby

49 Winter perch-fishing at a weirpool.

and Nobby lures, the Abu Atom and Little Wiggley spoons and, where the water is really deep, a Shakespeare Geneva spoon. The last-named is heavier than most we use — but it is probably the most compact wobbler in its weight/size ratio. Gladdings Flectolight and Mepps Rainbo bar spinners in large sizes have proved excellent in stillwaters, and are probably the most 'gaudy' lures that we use for perch, despite the general doctrine that one should use a flashy, showy spinner at all times.

With large waters we use the countdown principle of spinning. Once the bait has hit the water we count off a few seconds and then retrieve. We then repeat the cast, adding one or two more seconds to our counting after the bait has reached the water, thereby increasing the depth to which it will sink before we wind in. By casting fan-wise from the rushes or reeds at the left side of the water through 180° to the bank on our right, and counting before we start the bait working, we will eventually find the depth at which perch are feeding, besides carrying out a systematic search over the likely areas.

Often we locate a shoal and then find that we get lots of bumps at the lure, but no fish on the strike. Occasionally this is caused by fish hitting at a swivel or anti-kink device, in which case the cure is to remove it or use a smaller one where this is possible. Another reason for this behaviour is that perch will often hit at the lure broadside-on or from ahead, thereby missing the hooks. We have especially noticed this behaviour when using bar-spoons, and have a pretty fair idea that fish are actually going for the revolving blade itself and travelling at an oblique angle to do so. The only cure we know, when this happens consistently, is to increase slightly the rate of wind on the retrieve so that perch finish up chasing and hitting the lure from astern.

Yet another problem we have had is with foul-hooking, usually under the jaw. Again, we think that this is a question of too slow a retrieve, with fish accelerating beyond the hook to grab at the body of the spinner. Speeding up the retrieve helps, so does a change to a large single hook instead of the treble, or occasionally reducing the size of the lure itself so that it becomes a single mouthful. Mostly, these problems occur in running water, where any current helps the spinner to revolve faster than one is used to in stillwater. One feels this increase through the rod and tends to slow the retrieve to get the lure back to its imagined normal rate of spin.

With one possible exception, striking is hardly necessary when perch spinning. Providing that hooks are regularly sharpened, a light pull back on the rod to tighten the line is sufficient to drive the point home. Anything harder is asking for damage to the soft tissue of the mouth and the hook to tear free.

Our exception is when we are wobbling a small deadbait on the sink-and-draw principle — something particularly deadly between weed beds when any attempt to spin an artificial lure would lead to disaster. Minnows or sprats threaded onto the line (we rarely use a trace when perch spinning) with a single treble at the vent and a small weight in the mouth can be worked up and down through the smallest area clear of weed.

Once the cast is made, the rod tip does the work, raising the bait and allowing it to wobble slowly down again. It is when the bait sinks that the take usually occurs — and it is not felt until the rod tip is raised again. In that short time a perch often realises the deception and is on the point of expelling it as resistance is felt. Only a short, sharp strike will save a lost fish under these circumstances.

Getting perch to feed by artificial means is not impossible. Given a large area where fish are spread one can use a very fine, powder type of groundbait that will draw small fry together. This congregation will pull perch in to investigate and feed — evidenced by cartwheeling of the smaller fish as perch lunge through the shoals. This is the time to start spinning with a very small bar spinner, or better still a natural minnow.

Our latest experiment in perch fishing which so far has been extremely successful is with what we call the spinner cocktail. We make no claim to have originated the idea — it has been the vogue in America for a number of years. The American anglers attach strips of pork or bacon rind (it is sold ready preserved in packs) to the trebles at the tail of a lure and then spin with it in the normal way. We have not gone so far as using bacon rind (yet!) but have found that worms — red or small lobs — head hooked on one or two points of the treble, certainly do improve results. We have thoroughly combed an area where we know good fish to have been in residence without the cocktail and then mounted the worms and spun again only to connect with good fish.

Why? Well, we don't know. To all intents and purposes the trailing worm merely follows the path of the lure in front. But perhaps there is a scent of some sort that perch pick up and are attracted to. Come to think of it, weed caught around the trebles and trailed in a like fashion has never aroused attention, so that would seem the most logical conclusion. Anyway, next season we intend to start using strips of fresh-killed fish, rather in the fashion of the strip of mackerel attached to the sea spinner lures. Which highlights the whole beauty of perch fishing

50 Foul-hooked perch — the result of the perch striking high?

with a spinner — there is always some new approach, some new and untried idea with which to tempt this sporting fish.

Our last thoughts on perch concern night fishing. We had never stopped to give it serious thought until we picked up reflective types of lure, which sowed the seeds of the idea in our heads. We experimented, and certainly it is a successful method within certain limitations. First of all, we must define night. We have had no success in the middle hours of darkness, say between midnight and 4 a.m. And definitely no success other than in the more open months of the year, June to early October, when there is the very long dusk period and an early false dawn.

This proves pretty conclusively that there has to be *some* light available to reflect off the lure. We have also found that areas where perch are conditioned to artificial light — lakes and river banks beside a road, or where a bridge with street lights crosses the river — are far better bets than the waters where natural light only is available. Further, it pays to have a very sound knowledge of the area you are going to fish; distances are deceptive in the dark.

If you are going to night spin then our advice is to use a closed face reel to reduce any form of tangle which can be a nightmare in the dark, and pinch a small split shot eighteen inches or so above the lure. This will fetch up sharp against the top ring and prevent your winding the spinner up the rod. Our earlier advice of quality in casting and not quantity holds especially good here; in fact we survey the ground the afternoon before we night fish so that the majority of our casts are pre-planned.

Ken mentioned night spinning to Henri Limouzin, the celebrated French angling writer, during the course of a letter and it is interesting to note that his observations entirely agree with ours. Night fishing is

51 REFLECTIVE SPINNERS. 1. Mepps Aglia Rainbo. 2. Intrepid Flasha. 3. Intrepid Spinflasha (Red/Gold).

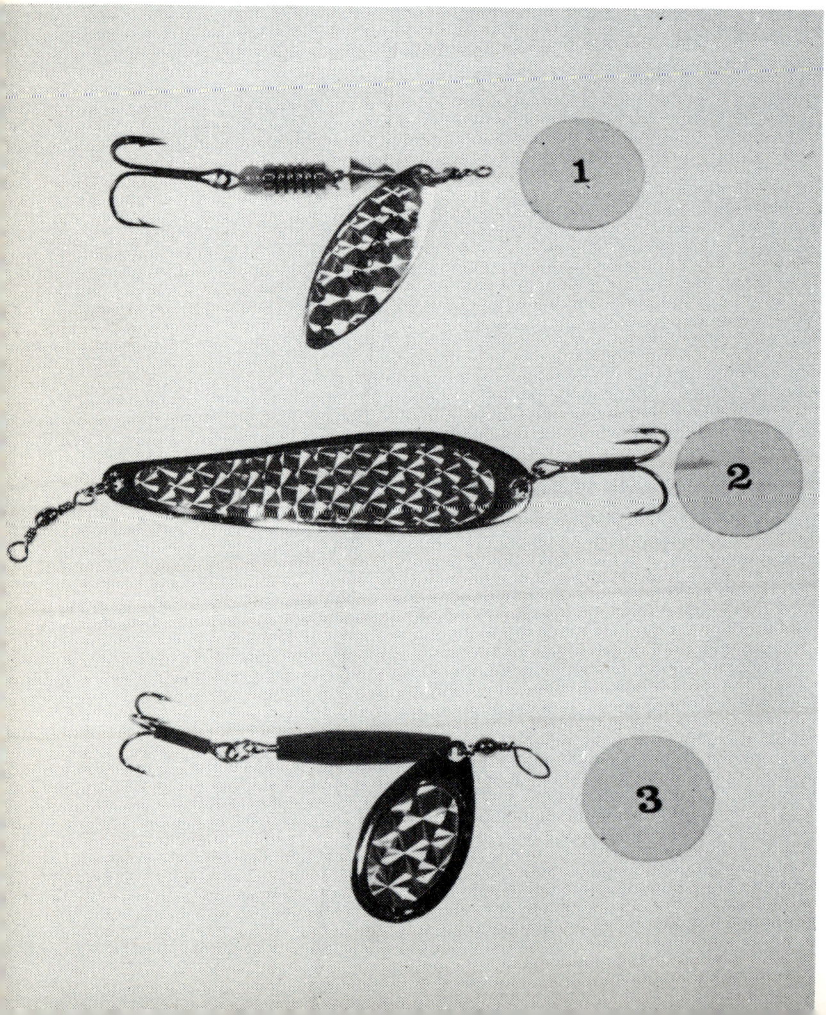

banned in France, but their very early and late fishing for perch, which overlaps into the pre-dawn and dusk periods can be excellent, and he also confirms our success with the Rainbo and Flectolite type of lure.

CHUB

Come summer or winter, rain or shine, hot or cold, the chub is a certain feeder open to an invitation of any sort from an angler. Long trotting, dapping, fly fishing, legering, plug fishing or spinning are all excellent methods that can be employed and, in the words of the immortal Bard, they all have their several exits and entrances.

We would be the last to suggest that it is possible to take a spinner and catch a chub on it every day of the week, anymore than the fly or trotted cereal bait would produce consistent results. But at certain times of the year and under favourable weather conditions a spun bait can be a very profitable way of fishing.

At what age chub turn cannibal is hard to tell. But it is interesting that neither of us has caught a fish smaller than 10 inches long by spinning, which would probably be in their fourth year and at a time when they are just about sexually mature. We believe that this size and sexual maturity link are important where spinning is concerned — because there is no doubt that the cream of the sport is to be found during the early part of the season, during June and July when spawning is taking or has just taken place, and enormous amounts of freshly hatched fry are present and spawning minnows or minnows on shallows.

It is during this period that chub move into fast water around weirpools and between narrow banks of a river where the current really speeds up. If you stand quietly using a pair of Polaroid glasses they can often be seen hunting and driving small fry as they dash across the shallows, in much the same way as perch and pike do. It would seem that, having spawned, they then set about systematically eating their own and every other fishes' current and previous season's offspring.

During those warm months we spin with the lightest possible tackle — until we developed the ultra-light rod we would use a No. 6 fly rod and fixed spool reel — and an assortment of matching spinners to comb the faster water. Deep spinning is definitely out where summer chubbing is concerned and, in direct opposition to perch fishing, the brighter and more flashy the lure the better the results will be.

Naturally, small fly-spoons are good except in the very fast runs, where they seem to get lost in the welter of foam and broken water. Mackerel spinners have turned up some good fish; their size/weight ratio is ideal, and if one stops fishing the lure it will sink with a wobbling action that can often pull a fish into making a take.

Mepps Mouche bar spinners with a fly tied on to the rear treble are absolutely grand fished in the 0 to 2 sizes. We have a very soft spot for Mouche Jaune that has a Palmer type fly body tied with a red tail. Also in the fly spinner category is the Abu Reflex bait, and the little Abu Fly, with nose mounted spinning vane to help keep an even body keel on the retrieve. Shakespeare's Marble spinner and its crimped blade reflect well, and the thin wire hooks are especially easy to drive home on the strike.

Our method of fishing these spinners is to cast slightly upstream and across, keeping the rod tip up and allowing the current to carry the bait below us, holding back so that the current does as much of the work as is possible. Once the bait is completely downstream we retrieve small amounts of line, allowing the spinner to hang and revolve as long as is possible. Naturally, if one can get on a weir platform, or the sill of the lasher, or on a projecting piece of bank, then the cast can be made to last practically indefinitely.

Never worry if the spinner is only in the broken water for a short time. Most of the fry and a large amount of the action will take place relatively close to the bankside. Which leads us directly to problems, for just because there is one devil of a lot of noise and confusion where fast water is running, it does not necessarily follow that fish can neither see nor hear you. A chub might be a big-mouthed bomb head, but he is probably the most cautious fish swimming where disturbance is concerned. You can hook and lose him without disturbing the shoal he has come from. But once you visibly or physically frighten one and he stampedes, then the rest of those near to him will follow suit – period. Keep low, keep quiet, and avoid sudden movement.

With the post-spawning period over, madness seems to go out of a chub's fish-eating habits. This does not mean to say that they are not as cannibalistic as before: it is merely that they will drop back into quieter water, using the very considerable amount of cover that a bank has to offer in the summer months. Small fish will continue to cruise around and can be caught relatively freely, but the better fish, appreciating perhaps that clear and low water has made them particularly vulnerable to danger, take up a stance with plenty of cover from reed, weed, bushes, trees and sunken branches around and over them. At this time they are at their most difficult to catch with a spinner. With legering, a lobworm could be anchored at the entrance to their shelter. With a plug, a small surface lure, it could be plopped like a falling insect directly into their safe area. But a spinner can only commit suicide when chub are positioned like this, as it frequently gets snagged.

The only hope that the angler has is to spin something close by that hold, so attractively that a fish could not help but swim out and intercept it. Instinctively one would think that this would be the situation for the spun natural bait, but our results have proved this to be far from the case; in fact spun natural baits for chub are, in our experience at least, the most unsuccessful. Other people have had a different experience; Dave Steuart, for example, has had lots of chub on the spun natural minnow.

One lure with which we have had success when attempting this type of spinning is the Devon minnow. The wooden or plastic types, about an inch to two inches in length, are light enough to spin within the top two feet or so of the surface and can easily be controlled by using the rod tip if snagging seems inevitable where a cast is misjudged. Colour seems to be immaterial. Ken favours blue back and silver belly, a combination he accidentally stumbled across when trout spinning on a well-known river. The trout just ignored everything that he fished, but the chub, three of which were taken from the same pool, left a welter of tree roots and literally smashed at the Devon.

Three other lures we have used to attract fish into open water have been the Mepps Mino and the Abu Drop-Fish and Morrum. The Drop-Fish and Mino are both artificial minnows perfectly reproduced in soft plastic, with a bar spinner mounted at the head. Although they are quite long, their weight ratio is low and they search the upper layer of water providing that the rate of retrieve is kept high. Fortunately, speed seems to be an incentive to chub at this time of year, in fact pulling the spinner up to the surface where it makes one hell of a clatter is a trick worth trying.

The Morrum is a lure we reserve for very deep holes where fish can be lying well down below the surface. Weight carried by this lure is in the artificial head which is made from lead, and the spinner blade is mounted behind it, making it also an excellent sink and draw bait. There are times when this scores, though in fairness we should state that most of our fish have been taken on the straight retrieve.

During the winter months chub tend to be taken more on the open

52 Mepps Mino — a small mouthful for a hungry chub.

river. Whilst they may use their summer areas as a retreat, fluctuations in water levels and temperatures can scatter them over a wide area that makes objective spinning very difficult. Most of our chub 'turn-up' at this time of year, often when we are perch spinning or spinning for pike with a small lure. From our fishing logs (we both keep one — they provide endless information and ideas over the season) we have noted that threc lures have provided most of our cold weather sport.

The Abu Droppen makes the best deep water spinner, an enormous weight ratio in the body helping the count-down method of spinning described in the perch section, besides ensuring that the lure works on an even keel. For working the middle and upper layers the Mepps Aglia has been successful — surprisingly in its largest (no. 5) size. This bar spinner and small Copper and Silvers have provided us with our only stillwater chub, taken on mild January days when pike were the objective. The fish took at the end of the retrieve, when the lures were being lifted from the water prior to re-casting, and it was thought they had followed them in over a considerable distance.

Our only spoon to meet with success in chub spinning has been the plain Copper and Silver type, unadorned, and fished slowly just over the bottom. It seems to do the trick after a prolonged period of frost and we have noticed that it is taken with only a little of a chub's usual smash-and-grab enthusiasm. Experimenting with our cocktail style in using small worms mounted on the rear treble has not been successful, which rather surprises us. But we have decided not to leave this idea, and there are fresh thoughts along these lines planned for next season.

There is one final suggestion we would commend to anyone who is thinking seriously of spinning for chub; consider the use of a boat. Boats and chub spinning are not usually associated, yet without a boat one is always looking regretfully at a small stretch of water that just cannot be covered because of an obstruction either on your side, or on the opposite bank. There are times when you can use only a few angles in retrieving a lure — usually those obliquely across the area that you want to cover — and how often has the angler wished that he could cross over to the opposite bank to cover a fish unapproachable from his position on the bank!

The independence that a boat can bring when chub fishing, the ability to drop quietly downstream covering either bank or both from the same position, the chances that are given to spin at any one of several angles to reach a fish, make the financial and physical efforts required to get a boat on the water more than worthwhile.

13

Spinning for other species

Barrie's best bream on spinner (Mepps) went $6\frac{1}{2}$ lb, and on one occasion he had several 7 lb plus bream fall off a 6-inch Jim Vincent spoon. This was in Ireland, but in Fenland he took three bream averaging $4\frac{1}{2}$ lb from a small drain in winter, two of which were fairly hooked with the tail treble of a Veltic in their mouths. His son Jeremy had a $6\frac{3}{4}$ lb fully scaled common carp on a $2\frac{1}{2}$-inch Veltic, this one being an autumn fish. Most anglers who do a lot of spinning will have caught the occasional carp species: barbel and tench, if not bream or smaller species. On the Continent large roach and hybrids are taken on small bar-spoons, and bream too. The question is, can the method be adapted in some way to make it more regularly productive? Various anglers have suggested that the use of very small spinners of the bar-spoon type might be productive, but it is not something which has yet caught on.

If we look at the problem from another viewpoint we may get a clue or two. Fly fishing has long been known to catch plenty of carp species: rudd, dace and chub in particular, but the advent of reservoir trouting and the use of fast stripped lures and large flies, has opened up yet other possibilities. Probably most anglers will have heard of the bream catches from Grafham water, made by trout anglers, and these were not small bream either. Now some of these large 'flies' are rather plug-like, and others have enough flash in them to resemble tiny spinners, so it may well be that tiny bar-spoons, with single hooks, could prove very attractive to the larger specimens of the carp family. However, it would be difficult to fish such spinners on fly tackle, and ludicrous to fish them on the spinning tackle normally used by anglers after pike, or even perch. What is needed is the ultra-light approach (chapter 10), using lines in the 2-4 lb b.s. bracket, no traces, and tiny spinners. We have had some extremely light but steely rods made in recent years. They are a delight to use, and with this equipment we have hopes of a much greater variety of species. It might be added that the kind of fixed spool reel you need for this fishing is one of the tiny but well made types — a small Shakespeare for example, or a Mitchell 408. The places to try are the known shoaling areas at the beginning of the season, or likely holes in a variable river. So far we've had a lot of perch and chub.

On the Continent, zander fall regularly to artificial lures, including flies, but in this country spinners have not to date proved very effective, even less so than plugs, and only occasionally do the fish go hard on them. Even then, 'mad' is a relative term, and the most Barrie has seen has been five fish in two days on bar-spoons, although he has had an unconfirmed report of up to five in one day, again on a bar-spoon. Bearing in mind that spinning is an accepted and successful technique in Scandinavia, and the amount of spinning done in Fenland, one wonders why the returns are poor. The only thing we can suggest for the real spinning fanatic is to concentrate on one of the smaller Fenland rivers such as the R. Delph. The tackle: as a starter anyway, a light 8-9 foot fast taper spinning rod; 6 or 7 lb b.s. line; long, thin, silver spinners, and a very fine, black, wire trace.

Henri Limouzin tells us that in France the zander, an increasingly popular fish, is not systematically fished, mainly because it is difficult to tempt them on spinners. In strange contrast the biggest zander caught in France, at weights of over 20 lb, *have* fallen to spinners and not to natural baits. The most successful anglers are those who fish slow and deep, and those prepared to risk fishing amongst submerged branches, trees and roots. Clearly there are strong contrasts between one country and another, France being roughly half way between Holland and Scandinavia on the one hand, and Britain on the other, so far as zander catches are concerned.

PART FIVE

Spinning for game fish

Contributed by
Dave Steuart and Fred Taylor

14

Spinning for trout

by

Fred J. Taylor

STILL WATERS

The late, great, Oliver Kite is reputed to have referred to still water trout fishing as 'spinning with a fly rod'. If he did (which I doubt) he was almost certainly referring to that branch of still water trouting which involves the casting and retrieving of flies dressed to look like minnows or the fry of other species. Oliver Kite was also credited with those immortal words, 'Chuck it out, pull it back and when you can't you've got one!' If he did, in fact, make such a remark (and I'm sure he did!) he was obviously referring to the use of the above-mentioned lure-type flies.

I would hesitate to disagree with Oliver Kite, and on matters entymological I would not do so at all, but there *is* more to lure fishing for trout than he would have had us believe. True, if you do no more than chuck-it-out-and-pull-it-back, you'll catch trout often enough to regard it as a reasonably effective method. But, although the casting of lure flies with a fly rod and traditional fly tackle requires a degree of skill, it does not take too long to reach a state of reasonable efficiency. Having cast the lure, however, the speed and manner of its retrieve probably require a little more than the sheer mechanical expertise needed for casting. Which is why, generally speaking, the fly-only ruling applied to most still water trout fisheries borders on the ridiculous.

If we accept the fact that 'flies' tied to represent small fish are strictly lures, and if lures, as suggested elsewhere in this book, are objects that flutter, spin, wobble or move in a manner attractive to bigger fish, why should we not be allowed to present those flies with a spinning rod and a casting reel?

Most of the trout fishing available to the average angler today is conducted on a daily permit, put-and-take basis. Waters are stocked, bag limits imposed, records kept and generally speaking it all works very well.

But why, I wonder, do public bodies controlling vast acreages of trout water which they claim to be 'open to the public', almost invariably enforce the fly-only rule? They have stocked their waters with trout, and now advertise the fact that they have, this year, introduced X number of browns and Y number of rainbows averaging so many pounds or parts of a pound apiece. They seek to attract the customers, to collect the revenue, to give sport to those who like to catch trout, to run and maintain good fisheries, and yet, despite their claims to be 'open to the public', they cater only for a small minority of the anglers in this country.

What of the angler who has no fly rod, no desire to purchase one and neither the wish nor time to learn the basics of fly casting? There is no way he can fish these so-called public waters because for some obscure reason his spinning tackle is strictly taboo.

It so happens that I *do* have a great deal of fly tackle, and despite the fact that I am not an expert fly fisher, I manage to catch my fair share of trout each season. What's more, I enjoy it, and to my way of thinking that's what fishing is all about, whatever the species. But not everyone *enjoys* fly fishing, and there are many situations where more pleasure could be achieved from the use of other tackle were it allowed. For the life of me I cannot figure out why spinning should *not* be allowed on *all* these public waters.

I've been told a hundred reasons of course. Fly fishers have argued emotionally but quite illogically about 'sporting methods' and 'unsporting methods', and I've listened to passionate outbursts from time to time about so-called 'unsporting tackle'. But I wonder. How can a method or a piece of tackle be sporting or unsporting? Only at the hands of someone who is not himself a sportsman can a method or a piece of tackle be put to an unsporting use. (Even a leister is not unsporting if it's propped up against a tree!)

Is it any more sportsmanlike to stand up to your thighs in water punching out a 10-yard, high-density shooting head with a lure fly on the end than to flick out that same lure fly on — say — a 2-ounce spinning rod with a swan shot pinched on the line to aid casting? There are many situations where the latter presentation is likely to be more effective, less likely to spoil the pleasure of others, and much more enjoyable to practise. And whichever way the trout happens to be killed, it's worth remembering that it's still a dead trout!

I've heard it said that if spinning was allowed, anglers who practised it would get their limits too quickly. So what? If that is their pleasure, and provided they do not fish on or return hooked fish so that they may continue to exploit a situation, what's wrong with that? It's unlikely to happen very often, and it wouldn't make any difference anyway on a properly controlled fishery. If someone wants to get a limit and be off the water quickly, that's his business. If he can seek to do it with a fly rod, why not with a spinning rod?

I've also heard it argued that, in any case, a good man with a fly rod will outcast and outfish a spinning enthusiast nine times out of ten. I think that is probably very true, and all the more reason, in my book, for relaxing these method restrictions. The whole business is quite illogical.

'If we allow spinning we shall upset the fly fishers,' one fishery manager told me.

But why? And what about the other anglers who are already upset about a situation which virtually bars them from fishing these public waters? Is it not possible to set aside certain areas for both methods? A short stretch of bank for light spinning, the remainder for fly fishing? And strictly to enforce the ruling that these areas are reserved for the methods nominated? That is important.

If I'm trying to cast and fish a nymph, I do not want someone beside me hurling out a spoon; but by the same token, if I'm delicately casting my tiny $\frac{1}{32}$-ounce lures on my little spinning wand, I don't want someone beside me ripping the water open with a number 10 shooting head!

In its wisdom the Thames Water Authority has already experimented with 'all-method' waters. It is hoped, after a suitable period, to be able to compare the effectiveness of different angling methods, and *then* to decide upon policy, rules and regulations. A sensible attitude.

It has been suggested to me by those in control of certain fisheries that spinning areas would *not* be taken full advantage of and that this would result in less space for the fly fishers, but so far it has not been put to the test. If, after a given period, it was found that the spinning sections were not being exploited, there could be no argument; but I do not believe this would be the case. I do think, however, that a great many anglers using the spinning sectors would eventually take up fly fishing!

I think we might see a situation develop where a spinner, having all but taken his limit in the morning, might well spend the rest of the day with a fly rod. Alternatively, the fly fisher, having flogged away nearly all day for no reward, might feel justified in having the odd hour on the spinning sector in the hope of catching the brace of fish he's rashly promised his neighbour!

I'm quite certain in my mind that the overall result of such administration would be an increase in the number of fly fishers and an increase in revenue for the public undertakings generally.

A few snobs might stay away in protest, but snobs are unlikely to be true sportsmen and they would not be missed! They never tried spinning for trout, but they're prepared to condemn it out of hand. I *have* caught trout by *all* methods and many experiences have proved interesting. Henry's Lake in northern Idaho for instance holds large numbers of remarkably big trout. The fishing there is free. Facilities such as boat hire, cabin rental, etc., have to be paid for, and a state licence is required before the water can be fished. The money from the state licence is used for conservation generally, and it would seem that this fabulous water is very much self-supporting in the way of fish stocks. The rainbows and cutthroats hybridise and grow big; stocks take care of themselves.

Henry's Lake is referred to often by Americans as the 'fish factory', and yet there is absolutely no restriction on method. You may float fish with worms, bait cast with plugs or spoons, leger with cheese, troll or trail with minnows and, if you like, you can buy salmon eggs for bait from the local store!

It's quite the most exciting fishery I've ever visited. Spinning is widely practised but it happens to be a fact that over 90 per cent of the fish caught there are taken on fly! They are caught that way because for the most part it is the deadliest way of catching fish from that water. The spinners have been quick to learn this, but other methods are still permitted. I imagine it will always be so. There are times when the spinners have a ball but any suggestion of 'slaughtering fish' is taken care of by the bag limit imposed.

There have been times when great slaughter has been brought about by fly fishers over here, but there has never been any suggestion of banning the fly! The petty rules and restrictions applied on reservoirs and public waters, where the object is supposedly to attract customers, give pleasure and derive income, have done much to maintain the great wall between coarse and game fishers that has existed throughout this century.

In fairness, however, it must also be said that the development of these public waters has done much to break down the barrier. By now it should have been flattened!

Is it not a pity that we cannot all fish as we would like? To enjoy experimenting with methods and presentations? To be able to put our thoughts and ideas into action without fear? To be discouraged from 'bending' the rules without actually breaking them?

The list of forbidden methods increases, and pretty soon we shall be unable to experiment at all. If that happens there will be no more pleasure left in the sport of fishing for me and hundreds like me. That's the part of it all that worries me.

Don't misunderstand me. I *do not* wish *always* to spin for trout, but I would like to feel I could do so as and when I felt so inclined. I would like that freedom because I happen to know that there are situations where it is warranted, and where it could do no harm whatsoever.

Thankfully, a few places remain where spinning is not a dirty word and, of course, if we forget those put-and-take waters, which provide an exciting but nevertheless somewhat artificial kind of fishing, and look further afield to the lochs of Scotland, and the loughs of Ireland, there's a wealth of stillwater spinning to be enjoyed. Strictly speaking, of course, lochs and loughs are not still waters but for the purposes of distinguishing between them and rivers I will refer to them as such. And, although the fish in these wild waters are produced naturally and without the help of stew ponds and trout pellets, there are certain similarities in their behaviour. In very hot weather, for example, the big browns tend to lie deep, and although I do not pretend to know why, there seems to be a certain magic about the 40-foot depth layer. Fred Buller, using char rigs and trailing fly-type lures at depths of up to seventy feet caught a number of big brown trout at the 40-foot level.

Similar results have been achieved in other waters, both here and abroad, and it seems utterly ridiculous to me that I should be forced to fish for these deep-lying brown trout in our put-and-take reservoirs with traditional fly tackle. There is no possible way of getting a fly down to that depth and fishing it in a manner likely to attract trout. It could be done with spinning tackle from a boat, and I see no reason why deep trolling with big spoons, plugs or spinners should not be allowed. These lures could be used with appropriate leads and where necessary, to reach extreme depths, modern down-rigger equipment could be used. Deep trolling with down-riggers is not a particularly exciting way of fishing until the actual moment of contact. Then it becomes something else!

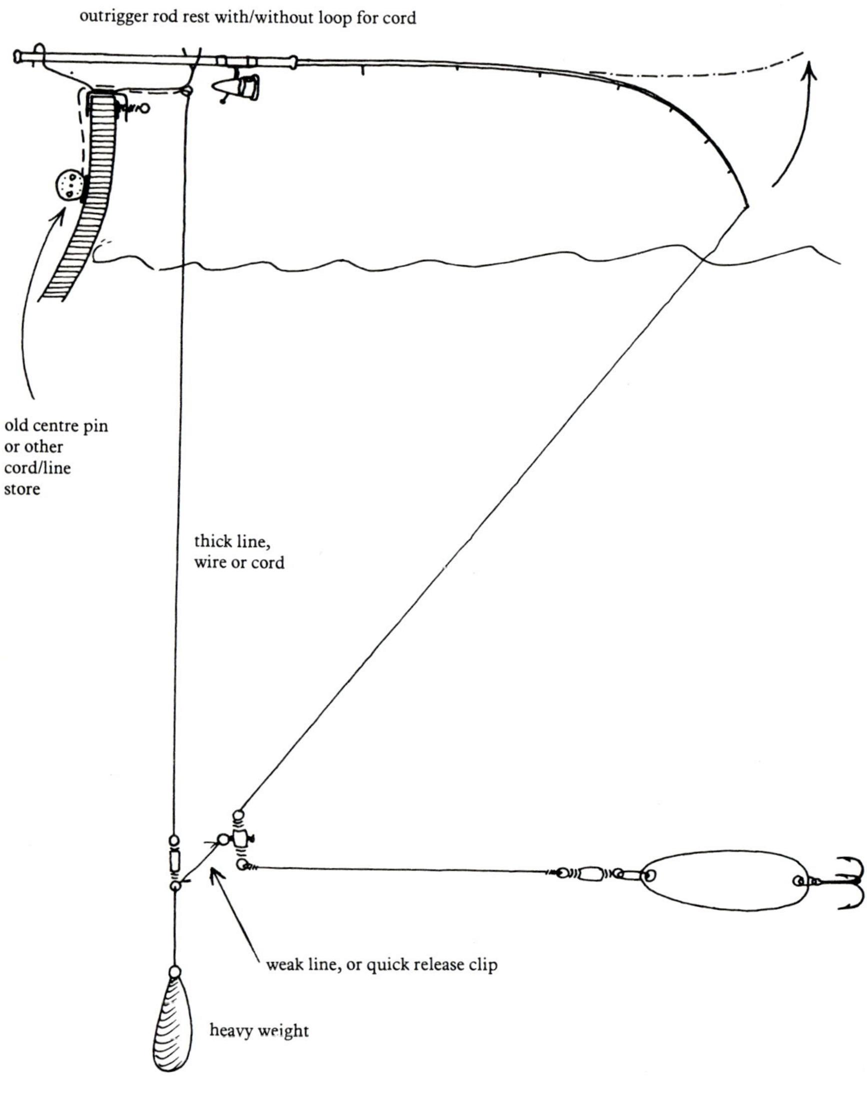
outrigger rod rest with/without loop for cord
old centre pin
or other
cord/line
store
thick line,
wire or cord
weak line, or quick release clip
heavy weight

Fig. **I**

It works extremely well on the Irish loughs and I've no doubt it could be made to work very effectively in our deep English reservoirs. The diagram (Fig. I) shows roughly how it works. The plug, spoon, spinner or feathered lure is taken down in a quick release clip attached to a heavy paravane-shaped lead weighing several pounds. This lead is attached to a wire line and is lowered by means of markings (or a sophisticated depth-counter) to the appropriate depth. The lure works happily in its wake but, being attached to an otherwise completely unfurnished rod and line, it breaks away from the release clip when a trout hits. The lead remains at the right depth, the fish is played to the surface on the light, limber spinning rod and the lure is sent down again on a new release clip with a free-sliding ring attachment. All very uncomplicated *once* the rigs have been set.

Speed of the boat is important and must be allied to the lure's action and the mood of the trout. Only experience can tell you when the boat is moving too quickly or too slowly. It takes time and patience, but it *is* rewarding, and there's more than a fair degree of skill involved. You have to be more of a boat handler than a rodsman, but it all 'comes good' with practice. It is, I venture to say, the *only* way of coming to terms with big deep-lying trout in any vast still water.

The dam ends of many English reservoirs are so placed as to make fly casting impossible. The high wall behind allows no room for an extended back cast, the deep water immediately to the front cannot be exploited to the full with fly tackle. It is, however, an ideal spinning situation, and where it *is* allowed there is no better method for exploring the depths.

The techniques of spinning, rates of retrieve, how plugs and other lures work, have already been explained in other chapters. There is no need for me to elaborate. I do not believe it's necessary to use huge lures (despite the fact that rainbows will take them) and I have long since come to the conclusion that a violent action on the part of the lure is often quite unnecessary.

I have my own fancies, fads and favourites. I've used them in the wild waters of the Outer Hebrides, the Rocky Mountains, the Canadian Wilderness, the Oregon desert, Ireland and in four of the American Great Lakes as well as our own English waters. I have caught, from these many places, brookies, browns, lakers, rainbows, cutthroats and hybrids – *all* on traditional spinning tackle used one way or another. I do not make this statement to prove what a clever angler I am because, truthfully, I'm not so smart. But I do want to make it clear that spinning *is* an effective and sporting way of catching many kinds of trout in many different situations.

For the record I prefer (and it is purely a personal preference) to use lure-type flies of one kind or other rather than bar-spoons, plugs, Devon minnows, etc. But because I have restricted myself voluntarily to lure-type flies made of hair, fur, tinsel, feather, etc., I've had to learn to dress them or arm them with sufficient *weight* to allow me to cast them with a spinning rod.

There are many ways it can be done and possibly the simplest is to have already made-up, a number of swanshots painted with black and white markings to resemble eyes. One of these can be pinched on to the line at the very point of attachment to the hook; it makes an ordinary streamer or bucktail fly look even more like a small fish, *and* it allows it to be cast on a light spinning outfit. Extra weight may be needed for longer range casting, and in my experience it is better to attach this in the form of extra swanshots pinched on immediately above and more or less touching the first (Fig. J). Uptrace leads will certainly add distance to the cast, but they give a strange feeling of being 'out of touch' during the retrieve. Somehow you're never quite sure just what the lure is doing when you've a chunk of lead between you and it. But with the lead bulked at the extreme end of the tackle (you may pinch shots on to the shank of the hook if there's room) there's a feeling of contact which is both agreeable and effective.

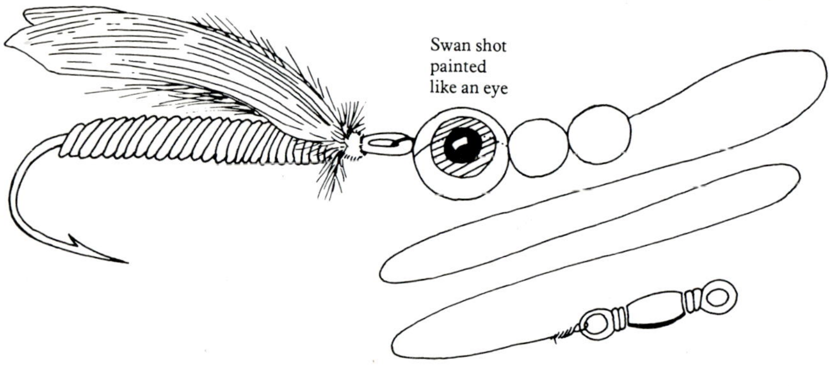

Fig. **J**

It doesn't take much imagination to dream up ways and means of making simple fly-type lures with weight built into them for casting purposes. There's no great skill involved (even I can make them) but they're fun to play around with; *and* they catch fish.

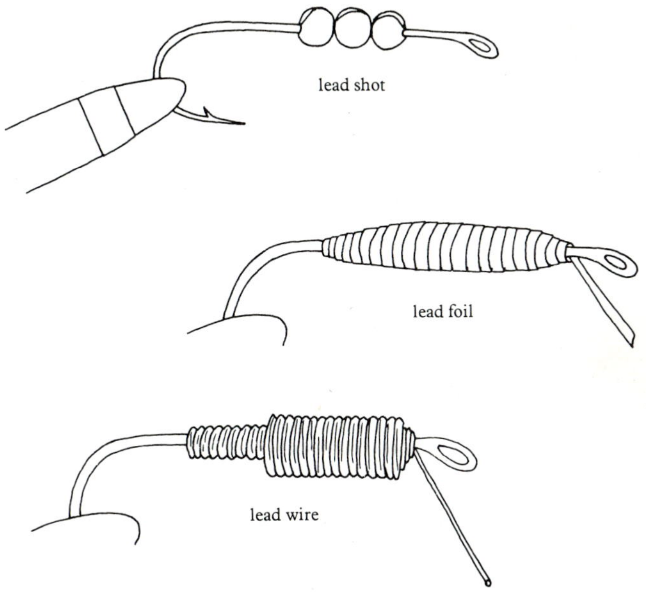

Fig. **K**

All kinds of coloured embellishments may be added to any of the weighted hooks shown (Fig. K) and I will not suggest any special dressings because they simply are not necessary. *Any* streamer fly dressing tied to one of these weighted hooks will catch fish on its day. Your problem is finding the right one for the day in question, but black, white, yellow and orange, or a combination of any two, are the colours I have found to be most effective.

Whichever way you choose to weight your hooks, use an Araldite-type glue generously in the process and let it set hard before adding the final dressings. Don't fuss about the dressing. It's easy to tie on a few more feathers or a wisp or two of hair when they've become worn. And remember too that very often these lure flies are most effective when they're well worn. They're often just 'coming good' when it's time to discard or re-dress them.

The diagram shows a fly vice being used to make up these lures, but you can work miracles with an ordinary pair of tweezers and a cotton reel. Think about it. Slide the cotton reel up the tweezers and the jaws will close tightly enough to hold almost any size of hook.

All this has little to do with the actual casting and retrieving of lures with a spinning rod. It has little to do with the playing and landing of trout, but you have my word for it that the lures I'm describing here *will* work excellently with a lightweight spinning outfit and that they *will* catch fish.

It's difficult to sit at a desk and tell someone *how* to fish, but I believe it *is* possible to pass on general information on *what to use.* These little snippets of information have been accumulated over many years of what I call open-minded angling. I do not believe they are common knowledge and I welcome the opportunity to pass them on, knowing that they have served me well in the past.

This is no place for a deep study of depth and temperature, but any observations in this particular field should be duly noted and allied to the speed, action, depth and colour of the lures being used. I cannot say: 'Do this when conditions are thus'. If I did it wouldn't work. All I can say is, 'Take note, experiment, and learn to put two and two together.'

There are, of course, many other factors to consider when fishing deep, still waters for trout, but again, observation is probably more important than technique. Finding fish, even without the restriction of the fly-only rule, is not always easy.

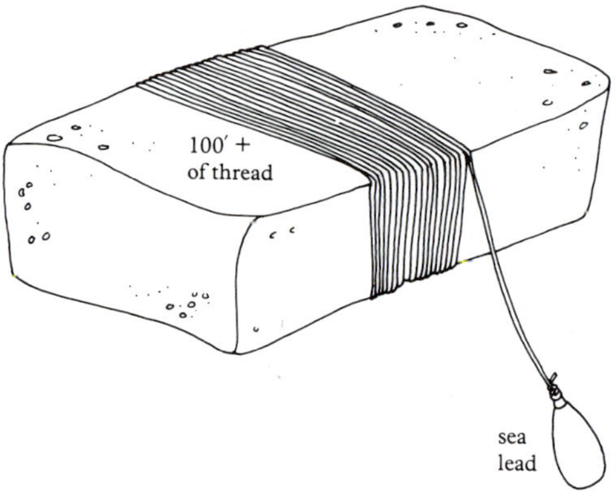

Fig. **L**

Catching one fish does not necessarily mean others are present, but it's at least a possibility. If you have caught a trout from — say — a drifting boat by casting a $\frac{1}{16}$-ounce lure, do you *know* at what depth the lure was working? After the fish has finally come to net do you *know* now exactly where you hooked it? You'll have drifted some way since it happened; can you now go back to the same spot again? If you are trolling (or trailing) a spinning lure behind a boat (allowed on some waters and certainly encouraged in many Irish loughs and Scottish lochs) are you certain you know the depth at which the lure is working? If you change it — will the second lure fish at the same depth, or deeper? Small points, but all-important regarding the whereabouts of fish.

Fig. L shows a simple marker for pin-pointing a 'taking spot'. Immediately a trout is hooked, toss it over the side of the boat. Its oblong shape ensures that the weight will keep stripping off the line, turning the block over and over until the bottom is reached. Then it will stop and no more line will be pulled off. The 'buoy' will rest immediately above the lead and mark the spot with deadly accuracy.

Big Irish and Scottish waters will be easier to understand if a transistorised sonar unit is put to use. Depth is then accurately recorded, but a simple way to ascertain the actual depth at which a lure is fishing is to row deliberately over a known shallow area and judge from what happens there. You may be surprised to find that your lure is fishing not eighteen feet as you'd thought, but less than half that depth!

There's much more, of course. I could go on discussing still water trout from now to eternity, but I'd probably be repeating some of the basics of spinning already dealt with in other chapters. I hope, however, that I've given you something to think about if and when the opportunity to spin for trout in still waters comes your way.

RIVERS AND STREAMS

The traditional way of spinning for trout in rivers is to tie on a small bar-spoon with a violent, vibrating action, cast it upstream and retrieve it slightly faster than the current speed. These tiny bar-spoons, mostly of French, Swedish or Norwegian origin, work extremely well even when travelling with the current and they catch fish. Because they are armed with treble hooks, however, they tend to be hard on small trout; and in the event that it is necessary or deemed advisable to return an unwanted or undersized specimen, these three points of penetration often make the task impossible.

It depends, of course, on what you want from your fishing. If, as I have done many times in wild and desolate areas, you are fishing for breakfast to be cooked over a camp fire, every fish, irrespective of size, will count — until sufficient have been caught. Then the fishing stops and the feeding begins! Half a dozen gudgeon-sized brownies taste just as good as one half-pounder when they're on the plate with an equal number of bacon rashers!

If, however, you're out to catch a brace or two of fish over a certain size and have no desire to hang on to the smaller ones, spinning with traditional treble-hooked spoons is not the answer.

Some of the fly-type lures already described and also those shown in Fig. M(1) and (2) will be equally effective and less harmful to any fish that is to be returned to the water alive.

Another way round the problem is to snip off two points of the bar-spoon treble and fish with only one. Odd fish will escape and almost certainly some of them will be of a takeable size, but at least they will be there for another time. (Fig. N(2))

It is not always necessary to cast upstream to trout, however, and there are times when the action produced by retrieving *against* the current — i.e. by casting downstream and retrieving upstream, will prove to be a better proposition.

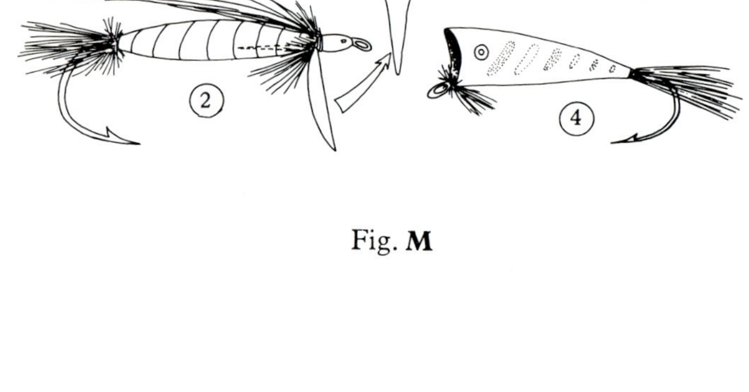

Fig. **M**

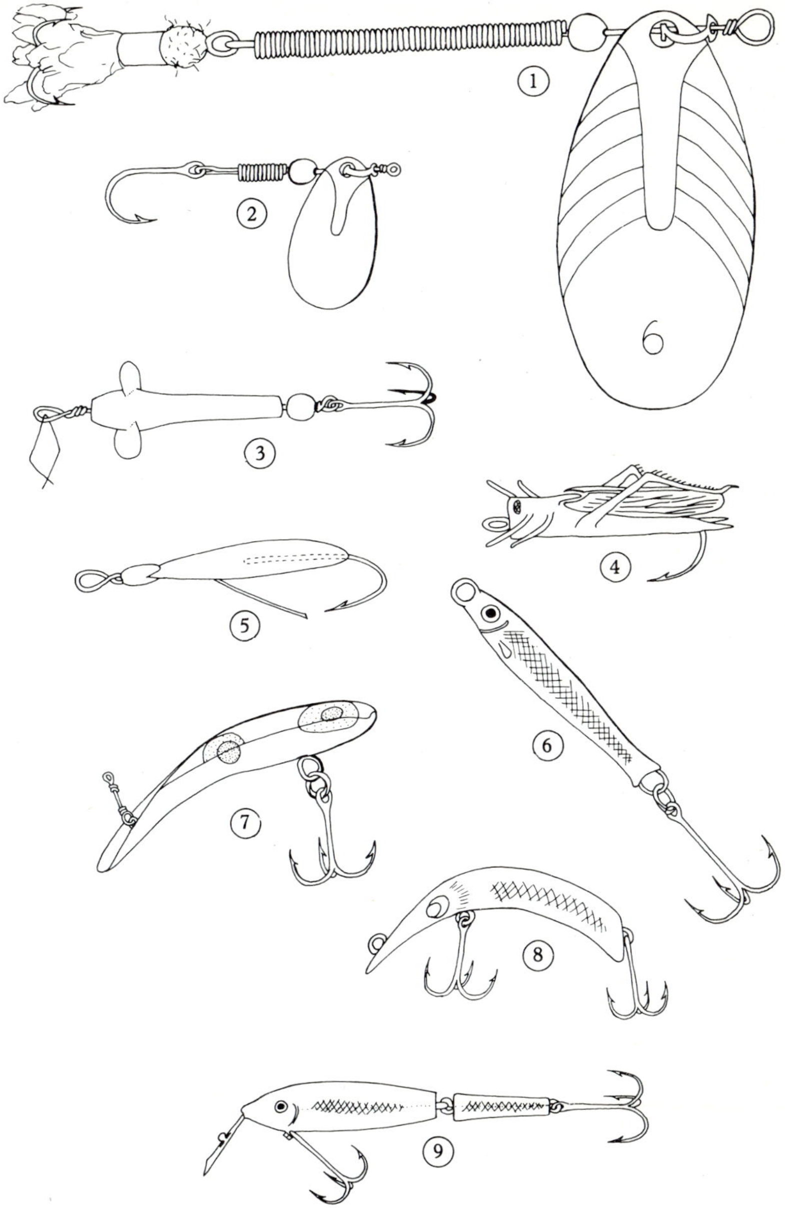

Fig. **N**

Remember one thing, however. Trout, like all other fish, spend much of their time headed into the current — which means that the downstream casting requires more caution on your part. You are more likely to be spotted when you are stationed upstream of a fish, but good use of cover and common sense will usually take care of that problem.

There are many tiny, overgrown streams where the trout are small and plentiful but which remain neglected by anglers either because their potential is not recognised or because the nearby salmon or sea trout are considered more worthwhile. Whatever turns you on! Me? I like to fish those waters. I like to get into the stream, work my way slowly up casting below the overhanging branches, flicking the tiny spoon or weighted fly into the likely looking spots. I like to force my way through the undergrowth and try some downstream casts through the areas I have not disturbed by wading, and while I will use fly and worm with equal pleasure if I think it is advisable, I often find the former quite impossible and the latter sometimes too easy. Worm-caught fish are also, in my experience, usually dead fish! There's no stopping a hungry little brownie from committing suicide! In these waters a half-pounder is a veritable monster, and I'm never really sure about what to do with such fish. Should I return them because they are so few and far between? Or should I retain them because they've reached their peak anyway? I can't advise anyone with regard to this problem— because I don't know the answer myself. I doubt, however, if it makes much difference either way.

Many of the big salmon rivers of Scotland are fairly stiff with trout, but it's a safe bet that those in the pools have seen every conceivable type of lure many times before! The gentle glides, the wide shallows and some of the big deep eddies hold trout in abundance however, and they will often respond to sensible spinning with ultra-light gear.

Again, the basics of spinning with ultra-light tackle have already been explained and there is little more to add.

The peaty burns of Scotland, the Welsh hill streams, the tiny becks of Cumberland all abound with small trout, and whether or not you regard the effort involved in catching them as a worthwhile occupation depends entirely on your own temperament. I do. And again, I like to spin for these fish with weighted fly-type lures. The fish are easier to catch with baits like small worms and maggots; but why struggle with what amounts to coarse fishing tackle when a tiny wand weighing a mere couple of ounces and a hatful of weighted flies will serve almost as well? Traditional fly fishing will catch these fish too, but again there are very few places where it can be practised.

53 Ken fishing for sewin on the upper reaches of the River Towy.

I hesitate to mention Thames trout because they are a breed of fish in a class of their own; but they are not extinct yet and every once in a while, a weir pool in the upper reaches produces a big brownie to a spinner. I have taken the odd fish from the Kennet on spun minnows and while these might possibly be regarded as Thames trout, I do not consider myself knowledgeable enough to delve deeply into the subject. I believe, however, that some of the weir pools are worth exploiting occasionally during the coarse fish close season if only to learn just how difficult a problem is presented!

Referring back briefly to the illustrated fly-spinners, Fig. M(1) is made from a long-shanked hook with a wire loop soldered on about one third of the way along it. The whole is weighted with lead wire and almost any kind of feather or hair will do for dressing. The important point about this lure is that the line is attached to the wire loop and *not* the eye of the hook. This loop must be bent backwards or forwards until the lure is seen to be wobbling rapidly in the current. You need to see this effect before you can appreciate its deadliness. Retrieve *upstream* for best effect.

Fig. M(2) shows a similar streamer fly with a wobbling disc (cut from an aluminium beer can) attached forward. Again, some bending and juggling is needed to get the required effect.

Fig. M(3) shows a simple popping bug. Not normally associated with trout fishing at all, it has, on occasions, proved extremely effective for rainbows in deep smooth runs during the so-called dog days of July. It is hardly a spinning-rod lure, but it can be cast downstream, allowed to float down even farther, and then retrieved with a series of 'pops'. Sometimes the effect is very dramatic.

The same lure used at night sometimes produces similar results, but Fig. M(4) shows an even better lure for that particular shady operation!

15

Spinning for salmon and sea trout

by

D. L. Steuart

SALMON

The first thing to understand when trying to catch salmon is that they don't eat in freshwater; they cannot, their stomachs won't allow it — so you're on a loser to start with! Having grasped this fact one can appreciate that it is factors other than the *necessity* to eat that causes a salmon to take hold of spinner, plug, fly, worm, prawn or whatever, whether it be a predatory reflex action, aggressiveness, territorial assertion, or downright stupidity. Our non-migratory species, will, when in feeding mood, eat a variety of foods, and depending upon quantity, the tiniest food forms to the largest they can swallow, and although conditions affect their feeding patterns to a certain extent, they have got to eat sometime and so are vulnerable to the angler. The 'prodigals', however, fat with excesses from 'overseas', and with stomach atrophied, have to be induced to take a bait* by the application of a well-known general procedure, based on the experiences of the past and present experts of the written word, and aligned to one's own lore.

This generally accepted basic set of rules is closely allied to water temperatures, for the obvious reason that all fishes' metabolism is tied to this, and in this respect a salmon is no different to any other fish. When the water is cold, and the salmon's metabolic rate is low, it has neither

* In this chapter on salmon spinning the word 'bait' means spinner of whatever type is being used.

the inclination nor the energy to move far for a bait, and so the salmon angler endeavours to present his bait as close as possible to the fish, at eye level. As the water warms and a salmon becomes capable of greater energy, the angler fishes higher in the water and generally a little faster.

The well known temperature of 48°F which most salmon fly-fishermen use as a guide to decide whether to fish near the surface with a floating line, or deeper with sunk line, can also be used as a guide by the spinning man to change his style or manner of presenting his bait. Some salmon fishers tend to use one method for the whole season, and doubtless lose some possible chances of a fish because of it.

There are reasons other than temperature, of course, for fishing with a certain size or type of spinner in a certain way, and I will try and elaborate on these by explaining why I use a particular method and bait as we explore the field of 'Spinning for Salmon'.

You cannot catch fish if you're not fishing where they are, so it is as well to familiarise oneself with the current speeds and river-bed contours where salmon like to rest, while awaiting conditions to urge them to move upstream. They generally like to lie in fast water, or appear to, in similar conditions to those one would associate with barbel swims. I say, 'appear to'. I have perceived that although a salmon is at first glance lying in fast, strong, water, it is usually positioned where a division of current or turbulence creates backflow, an easier flow in which the fish can maintain position with little effort. This can be seen when particles of detritus are travelling with the flow, and the behaviour of such matter is observed as it enters the salmon's 'lie'. However, as a generalisation, we look for salmon where the water flows fast.

The obvious lies therefore are the outside of bends, where the river flows strong and deep; in our southern rivers, often where piles have been hammered to contain the river by arresting bank erosion. Deep-cut banks caused by fast currents; narrow stretches creating a speeding-up of flow; gradients; all create possible lies. Fish* like to lie just upstream of a gradient where there is a pull over their backs as the flow accelerates, influenced by the increased velocity down the incline. Sometimes it is the tail of a pool — sometimes not, but a 'run-in' to a pool.

Dictated by the angle of the gradient, fish may or may not lie in the water flowing over them. It may be too fast, too turbulent, and without obstruction to create short-rest lies, as some rocky waterfalls give to ascending fish.

* In this chapter the word 'fish' means salmon.

The pool below a gradient will hold fish in various places, dependent upon its character. There could be fish lying alongside the main flow into the pool: if it is deep, they might lie in a back-current underneath the white water where it enters the pool, and not always near the bottom, alienating to flow. If the flow enters to one side of the pool they may lie at the current's edge or alongside the bank edge — smooth rock faces, piling, or straight-cut banking of any sort they favour, and will lie at all depths between the river bed and surface alongside these, again the depth at which they lie subjected by a flow to their liking.

Cover is important. Salmon will sometimes prefer lying in shallow water where there is cover, rather than in deep water where conditions would cause them to be easily visible, i.e. slow flows and gin-clear water. High banks will give cover, as will trees, bridges, and any overhang. Remove the cover as some misinformed anglers and fishery administrators are inclined to do, and you remove the fish.

Groynes generally create the conditions that fish like, but it is unlikely such features would not be recognizable even to the novice.

One very important consideration, as much when spinning for salmon as any other fish — *keep out of sight of the fish!*

It's about time we did some fishing.

Paternoster-spinning.

Early season fishing for 'springers' can be a hard, cold, fruitless job, but if successful, the prize is so great that all the effort and discomfort becomes well worth while. In my view, there is no other fish so beautiful and symmetrically perfect as a white-bellied, silver-flanked, steel-blue-backed, spring salmon. I live in the south, near London, and the nearest salmon fishing available to me is the River Test, the Hampshire Avon, and the Dorset Stour. All these rivers are fairly fast-flowing and gravel-bottomed, and when fishing for the few springers that still enter these rivers, from the opening day of February 1st for a couple of months or so, for reasons that I will explain later, I favour spinning paternoster fashion. This is a fairly simple way of fishing a bait very close to the river bed, a bait that travels very slowly through the spring lies.

Basically, terminal tackle is simple. The chosen line, 15-20 lb breaking strain, is tied to a ball-bearing swivel; a nylon trace approx. 3-foot long of the same strength as the line is attached to the other end of the swivel, and to the trace is tied a link swivel to attach the bait of your choice. From the top-eye of the ball-bearing swivel a 6-10 inch length of nylon hangs, of much lighter b.s. in case it gets snagged (I favour 6 lb b.s.), and to this nylon I tie a link for the easy changing of pear leads (See Fig. O). During the course of a day's fishing the pear lead size may be altered several times to counteract different pressures on the line of current speed and depth, which would cause a bait to travel too fast across the river, too high in the water, or in the case of too heavy a lead, not to travel across by the current's pressure on the line at all, but remain anchored. Lead size is all-important; don't be afraid of it. In some lies in heavy water you sometimes need 2 ounces or more.

The method of fishing is to cast across the river in a downstream direction at an angle of about 45°. Line is allowed to flow from the spool to shoot the lead to the 'bottom', the bail is closed (fixed spool reel) or the gears engaged (multiplier), and with rod held high, the tackle travels in an arc from its cast position to the near bank as the current pushes on the across-stream line, lead, and bait. The farther downstream one casts and the higher the rod is held, the slower the tackle will travel across, but avoid casting too far down — a very long line will make hook penetration more difficult.

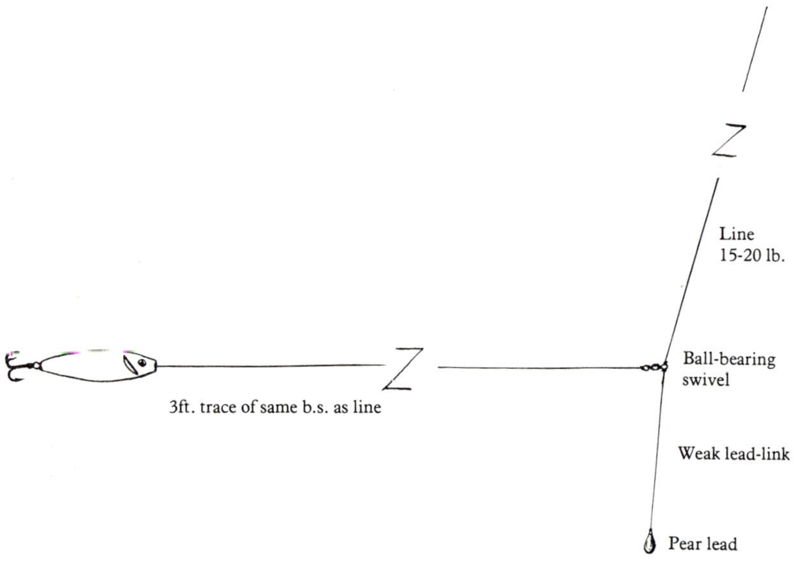

Fig. **O**

If lead size is right one can feel it dragging bottom as it comes over, and if it occasionally catches, a slight lift of the rod will free it to continue its journey. When the tackle reaches the angler's bank, it is rewound, the angler takes a few steps downstream, and recasts.

By this method the river is searched methodically yard after yard in the hope of putting the bait very close to the fish, right on the bottom, for as mentioned early on in this chapter, when the water is cold, as it is in early season, a salmon has neither the inclination nor the energy to chase a bait far or fast.

Salmon will enter a river readily enough in water at almost freezing point, 33°F anyway, especially on a spring tide, and will move slowly upriver until confronted by any obstruction such as a weir, waterfall, or any gradient that is steep enough to cause white water. In the cold water they haven't the energy to surmount difficult water, so if one is lucky enough to be able to fish the lower beats in early spring — especially the first major obstacles — before the water temperature rises to approximately 10°F above freezing, there should be a few new fish waiting to be caught by correct bait presentation. After the water reaches the low 'forties', fish will start negotiating falls and move upstream at a faster pace.

So we hope we are fishing water where early salmon have reached; we are using the paternoster-method as we know we must get down to the fish and fish slowly, and as fish may be very scarce we know we must search the 'ground' thoroughly, but what of baits? There are several considerations here and if we start with the salmon we realise that in its cold state it needs a jolt, a high impact to cause a reaction, and so we start with size — we use a large bait. We must then consider the water in which the salmon is lying. Is it clear or dirty, deep or shallow? We assume it is going to be fairly heavy, fast water, in February/March, the time of rains and melting snows, and we also take notice of that in our bait assessment.

Assuming rains have made the river a bit coloured, as well as needing a large bait, for the salmon to really get the message we need a bright colour. The Avon favourite is yellow; in devons, the yellow-belly, and in heavy, coloured conditions, I would use a $3\frac{1}{2}$-inch bait. There is nothing to beat a light wooden or plastic devon, for paternoster work. Any heavy metal job fished by the method would soon catch bottom and snag; the wooden devon however, in any situation where the current eases, instead of fishing deeper will float up and keep clear, and plastic patterns, Dibro for example, need such little flow to keep them working that they rarely ever snag either. Without wooden or plastic devons we couldn't fish a *short*-link paternoster with the bait only a few inches from the river bed, following the contours. As depth increases, the lead takes down the bait; as it shallows, the lead bounces up the slope with bait following instead of catching up.

In very dirty water the big 3½-inch yellow-belly is necessary even in shallow rivers to give enough impact, whereas in shallow water three foot or less, with just a touch of colour, I would either change down to a 2½-inch yellow-belly, or change the colour and retain the large size — brown/gold, black/gold — considering a 3½-inch yellow-belly to be just

54 Three nice fish on plastic devon.

too much on shallows, that might put a fish off. In deeper water with only a little colour, it would be as well to use the large size and bright colour while temperatures are low, as even slight turbidity causes a deterioration in visibility the deeper it gets, remembering it is 'impact' we are after.

In gin-clear water — and we've found this at the beginning of the season once or twice in recent years — I would still take my first consideration as read and start with a large bait, but a brown/gold, or black/gold, wooden devon, or a natural sprat, golden sprat, or what I call my kipper-devon. Natural sprats are soft, but mounted on a spinning flight (a celluloid-vaned flight is light enough to be used paternoster fashion) they catch salmon, *and* they smell nice. Golden sprat catches a lot of fish but I've never liked the smell much, although Ken and Barrie's method of de-form alinising might help in this direction. I've tried smoked sprat — they look O.K. and smell O.K., but break up. If you are lazy, stick with the sober-coloured devons, but for a change-bait that lasts I have recently been using my 'kipper-devon'. This is simply a celluloid-vaned flight with a devon-shaped length of cork glued to the mounting-pin. The cork is made slim to allow a wrapping of skin, taken from the flank of a lovely golden kipper. It is kept in place by a winding of elasticated cotton. The skin, shading from blue-black to golden, can be wrapped in such a way as to give the bait a dark back and a golden belly. It's a devon that smells nice, and when a fish takes hold, perhaps tastes nice. The cork body gives it buoyancy to fish paternoster style.

As the water warms — getting into the low forties — it is usually clearer, and with the fish a little livelier we cut down bait size to $2\frac{1}{2}$-inch, lengthen the lead-link a few inches to fish the bait a *little* above the salmon, and decrease lead size slightly so that the bait fishes across a mite faster. Bait colour is sober. But despite the salmon's slightly increased liveliness, if the river is still very coloured we return to the early method of big bait — perhaps 3-inch instead of $3\frac{1}{2}$-inch — yellow-belly, shorter lead-link, and fish very slowly. This is not so much for high impact, but to give the fish a chance to see the bait.

Later in the spring, when water temperatures are in the upper forties, we may dispense with the paternoster altogether and fish a different method, but will always return to it after heavy rains, when conditions dictate that we again have to put the bait right into the salmon's mouth.

A further point about fishing the paternoster when temperatures have reached the low forties and rising, and the water is clear; we can start increasing the number of steps between casts. The fish will see a bait farther away, and when in taking mood be prepared to move farther to intercept it or chase it, and so we can work through the river much faster. We can also confine ourselves to fishing the obvious lies that are appearing as the river levels drop — they're not always so easily read when the river is high, and then a fish could turn up anywhere! Going through faster, plus the lengthening of daylight, will mean that we have time to work through a pool twice. The second time through will sometimes produce a fish. Probably, first time through woke it up, and second time through decided its interest.

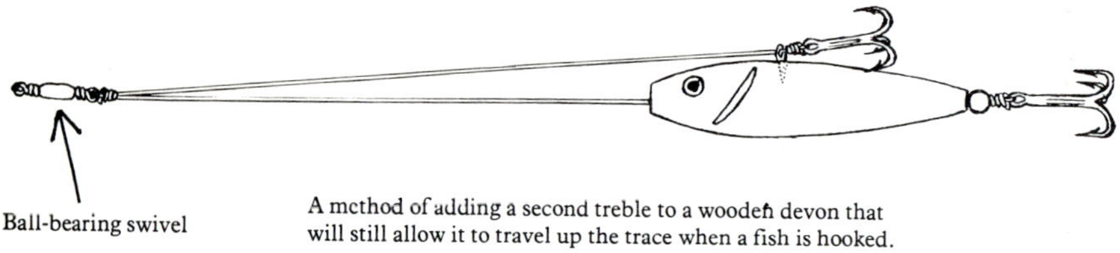

A method of adding a second treble to a wooden devon that will still allow it to travel up the trace when a fish is hooked.

Fig. **P**

I favour the paternoster and the light devons as *the* method for early season for so many reasons. It fishes slowly; it takes the bait right down to the fish; if the lead gets snagged the weak lead-link will break and the bait is retained; the bait rarely gets snagged; in the fast water of early season the devon does not create drag and increase speed as it comes across; it commences fishing as soon as it enters the water; being buoyant, the devon will spin even if the lead is allowed to act as an anchor to hold the bait in one position for a known difficult fish; it will fish right under the far bank by allowing the lead to shoot to the bottom upon entry, before the current acts on the line and brings it across; and it's the easiest of ways to correctly present a bait early season. When fish are scarce it can also be the most boring and tiring — what I call 'the hard flog of spring salmon fishing.'

Orthodox spinning

Unfortunately (or fortunately; depends how you look at it), it is not possible to use the paternoster in all rivers. In turbulent rocky rivers, small and large, much associated with salmon fishing, it is not practical to fish with a hanging lead, unless you own a lead mine, for it will continually be getting snagged. One then fishes in far more orthodox fashion with up-trace lead, Wye lead, or Jardine lead, and fishes as deep as possible consistent with keeping the tackle from getting snagged. I still favour the wooden or plastic devons and apply all the aforegoing lore as to bait size, colour, etc., but some anglers who know their rivers very well will use a heavy metal devon, with or without up-trace lead as conditions demand, knowing just how deep they can allow it to go, and just where to raise it out of trouble. The knowledge probably cost them dear at first.

With the wooden devon, if the lead is felt to touch bottom or rock, a slight lift to clear it should also lift the devon out of trouble.

The method of fishing is still across and down, trying to cover as much holding water as possible. I have the feeling that were it possible, the paternoster would outfish the orthodox in early season, although many hundreds of fish fall to the latter method. Compared to the rivers where we can fish paternoster-style, the others hold so many fish that sooner or later any method of bait presentation is bound to pass near a fool fish willing to take.

Long spoons and bar-spoons can be used to fish salmon early season in shallow streams by making a fairly long cast downstream, to fish them across as slow as possible. The trouble arises when trying to get them to go deep, especially bar-spoons. They create such a pull when fished downstream, that unless very heavily leaded they fish close to the surface. Such spoons are best left until the water warms up, when they can be fished in a different manner.

With river temperatures in the upper forties we can start on more interesting ways of spinning providing the water is a good colour — clear or just slightly coloured. With a slight colour we might still fish paternoster-style, but make our casts at a lesser angle downstream so that it will fish round faster. In clear water we can dispense with the link-lead and fish more orthodox with up-trace leads to devons, toby spoons, bar-spoons, wobbling spoons, plugs — anything that the angler thinks might interest a fish. Sizes of devons will have dropped to 2- or $2\frac{1}{4}$-inch, and other baits will range about that size, with wobbling spoons and plugs perhaps just slightly larger. Bar-spoons with their greater vibration impact can be a little smaller, although I personally will still use, say, a Mepp No. 5 Aglia in Avon or Stour where the fish run large. On the River Test though, I will drop to a size 4 during the same period, for the salmon are a few pounds lighter, so there we have yet another consideration factor in choice of bait size.

We might fish a few square casts so that the bait travels across as we *wind* back, controlling the fishing depth by rod angle and winding speed, with the bait coming across slightly downstream, and making an inviting turn as we wind when the bait has come three-quarters of the way across to the angler's bank.

Once temperatures have reached the fifties I will fish some of the day with Mepps or similar bar-spoons in preference to other baits, and do a deal of casting *slightly* upstream, winding back so that the bait comes across square to the current with the blade giving a broader image to the upstream-facing fish. One must fish small rivers very carefully when adopting this method for you are fishing for fish that are opposite you in the river, and careless movement on the bank or in the water, although it may not always frighten fish away, will make them nervous and unlikely to take a bait.

Upstream spinning

Providing the water is clear, the low fifties are also the river temperatures when I have the occasional throw directly upstream in fast water, winding back fairly rapidly. Although some anglers are under the impression that a fish has to move fast to take a bait coming downstream at speed, it is a fallacy, and requires less effort from the fish than the taking of a bait just dangled in the fast water. The fish seeing the bait coming down, may move its position slightly and simply intercept it with little effort, and even if it chases the bait downstream, no extra energy is required. If we assume the fast water is travelling at 4 m.p.h. and it needs a speed of 1 m.p.h. to work the bar-spoon, to make it revolve we must wind at a speed in excess of 5 m.p.h. But a fish travelling with the current has only to swim at a little over 1 m.p.h. to overtake the bait as the current takes it downstream. To take a bait dangled in the current it must swim at little more than the current speed.

Come the summer and low water conditions, very much more of my spinning is then directly upstream. There are, in my opinion, lots of advantages to be had by fishing in this manner, which increase as the summer advances. One of them, and a very important one where salmon are concerned, is that I seem to have a more successful number of landings to takes. I have always had a few salmon come adrift during the course of a season, and every salmon angler I know has similar experiences, so if casting up and winding down increases the chance of a hook taking a fair hold, it's very important.

If a salmon intercepts the bait as it comes down, the hook should lodge in a corner of its mouth; if it follows down and turns back as it takes, which salmon often do, the hold should also be in the scissors. This is a very secure hook-hold, although the 'kiting' effect of such a hold on a large, long-jawed, cock fish, can be a little disconcerting.

When a fish is hooked, the downstream angler is already in a better position for playing it from below, than is the angler who hooks a fish from upstream. The salmon will often take off upriver, and this gives the downstream angler the advantage of having the fish fighting the current as well as himself. If weeds have grown, there is less fear of entanglement in playing a fish from below; if weeds are abundant, it is often advisable to cast up and spin down the runs between them when it is not possible to fish downstream.

55 'Tis' a grand fellow ye are!'

If cut weed is coming down, providing it isn't too damn much, it is also feasible to get a few casts in by throwing upstream and winding down with the stuff.

Another advantage is that as the current bears upon the line, one can cast a longish line upstream to the far bank, and spin down that bank a long way before the bait leaves it and starts coming across. And because the bait will come down in a fairly straight line it is a very quick way of covering a lot of water, for the bait must have been seen and been in close proximity to all the fish, by casting up alongside the lies.

The depth at which the bait fishes can also be fairly easily controlled.

In the low fifties I will have used Mepp size 4, or 3 if very clear, with devons $\frac{1}{2}$- to 2-inches, and as I concentrate more on upstream work toward and during summer, I will have dropped to a Mepp 2. Should I feel like a change I use metal devons for their ease in casting up without up-trace lead. In very low water even a tiny 1-inch devon or no. 1 or 0 Mepp will take fish. These small baits can be cast to a fish several times without worrying it unduly.

Over the last couple of years when upstream spinning, if fishing a small bar-spoon where I have needed lead to aid casting, or to fish it deeper, I have placed the lead right down near the spinner to act as a head for the bait — like a Voblex. I have fished this way since having a hell of a pull when winding down fast, but not connecting. As I finished the retrieve I saw a salmon swimming down directly behind the up-trace lead and it occurred to me that on occasions when I have had a pull and not hooked the fish, it could well be a fish that hit the up-trace lead. When casting up and retrieving a bait and using an up-trace lead, the first thing the fish sees is the lead, and if it's really in a taking mood, it may well hit the lead before the following spinner. The trouble is, it rarely gives one a second chance!

It will be noticed that as the temperature of the river has risen through the year, so we have used smaller baits, fished higher in the water, and faster. As fish become livelier through the year, so they will refuse larger baits, or even be frightened by them. I don't pretend to understand this but have observed fish that have refused a bait, been rested, then taken a smaller one. Although I have caught salmon by continually casting to them with small baits, quite often continually showing them a large bait will cause them to move house.

There are many more observations one can make about salmon taking spinning baits. For example, fresh run fish will sometimes take a larger bait than fish that have been in the river for a while, and yet, toward the autumn, stale fish may well start hitting large baits again. In the latter case it could be an aggressiveness that becomes positive as the spawning season nears commencement, as I have watched cock salmon chasing trout and salmon parr off the reeds during cutting.

Small rivers

Fishing some of the smaller, natural, rocky rivers, often with heavily bushed and treed banks, does tend to cut down on one's ability to cover all the water where a fish might rest, but then such waters are usually fairly easy to read and the salmon lies rather obvious. It may be that one has only one or two stances from which to fish a stretch of water, and to cover it as well as possible will require upstream, downstream, and square casting, all from one position. This may mean adding or removing lead to cast to a new position and fish at the right depth and speed — not so critical later in the year in the small river, but

56 A brace to the Mepp 3.

57 A hook-hold here might not penetrate the maxillary and fall out.

important early in the season. This, I think, is why so many of the locals prefer worming — an art if fished well, and more certain of fishing right.

Some of the casting must be very accurate in streams, as when placing a bait into a small gap amid or beneath foliage on the far bank, flicking it across from amidst foliage on one's own side, or trying a long one upstream between branches that try and pluck at the offering with gnarled fingertips — sometimes successfully.

Such casting is much easier when all the weight is in one place — at the end of the line — so either use baits with sufficient weight 'built-in', or place the lead close to it, as I have suggested for upstream fishing. Some anglers like heavy metal devons for this sort of work, and catch a lot of fish on them too!

Temperature changes affect the fish of small streams more readily than in the larger river, as such changes can happen more quickly. A large river is less likely to be affected by a small change in air temperature, but the lesser volume of a stream may well be affected enough to stop fish taking, or start them showing an interest!

Hooking

I once saw three salmon holding station over eight feet of water. They were only some three feet below the surface, sitting comfortably on top of a backflow, although the current over their backs was fast and strong. I flicked a devon upstream of them, watched it come flickering downstream past them and saw the smallest of the three, a fish about 7 lb, swing out and follow the devon. As it swung round into the slack water the salmon closed its mouth over it. I did nothing except continue winding, expecting to feel the rod go down. In the same second as it took the bait the salmon opened its mouth and the devon came out *spinning.* I didn't feel a thing! The fish turned back to lie with the other two and showed no further interest. Although I intermittently tried various baits during the course of the day, all three fish took no notice, although in the evening the 7-pounder did take a prawn. Pity about the other two. One was about 20 lb and the other about 14 lb.

I have seen salmon swim up to a bait and knock it with their nose with mouth shut. I mention this and the previous instance to show that there can be problems with hooking salmon. Occasionally one gets a very sharp knock as a bait comes across, and I often wonder if it is a warning to the intruder to keep away, and whether a salmon does it with mouth closed. It always excites me anyway, as another cast to the same spot often results in a proper take.

The main difficulty lies in the strength of a salmon's jaw, for as in nearly all animals, the jaw muscles are the strongest. When a salmon takes hold of a bait and the angler strikes, I don't think he moves it within the fish's mouth at all and so doesn't drive in the hooks. Instead, the salmon feels the pull, opens its mouth and ejects the lot. When fishing down and across early in the season, and the salmon hasn't moved far for the bait and is probably still facing upstream while holding the bait, a good hook-hold is least likely. Later in the season when one is fishing square, faster, or upstream, when a salmon moves farther to a bait and then *turns* back to its lie, a good hook-hold is much more on the cards.

Some experts say that you should never strike, but let the weight of the fish set the hook, as it *will* turn away if it doesn't feel a pull. Some anglers I know, use very stiff rods and strike hard. I've tried both methods, but still fish fall off. Probably a delayed hard pull is best, but a quicker strike in summer when grilse are running — fish which are lively and eject a bait quickly.

Another problem is the long bait — devon, toby, etc. specially early in the season, or in dirty water when one is using large sizes. I'm positive that salmon often take hold crosswise, and with only a treble at the tail the hook isn't within the mouth of the fish. I have got over this problem a little by adding a centre-treble to some of my devons and spoons, but in a manner that still allows the devon to slide up the line out of the salmon's mouth when the fish is hooked, and for the spoon to swing free. A devon or spoon that remains in a hooked salmon's jaw may be waggled about in its effort to get rid of it, and so lever out the hooks (See Fig. Q).

If one is prepared to go to the trouble of replacing baits that continual casting will destroy, one way of overcoming the hooking difficulties to some extent is to use natural baits whenever possible. Natural sprat and a hard strike rarely result in a missed fish, as the soft bait doesn't stop the hooks moving when the strike is made. Golden sprat will last longer, as the formalin preservative toughens the flesh, but hooks can still be struck through it.

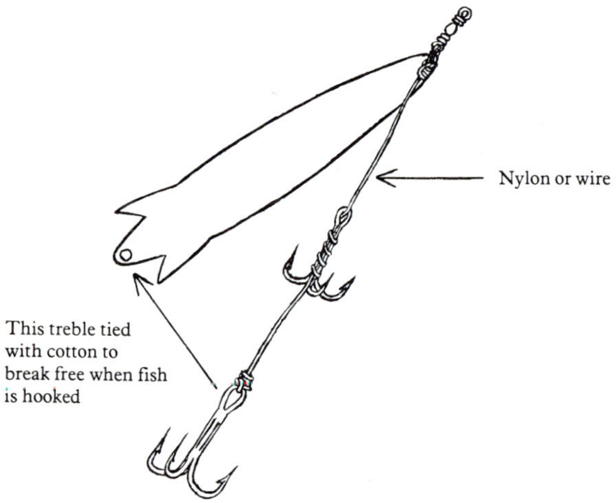

Superior hooking is possible with twin trebles
for fish that take crosswise.

Fig. **Q**

When a small bait is wanted, a natural minnow makes a good spinning bait although I haven't yet had success with it, but I haven't used it much for salmon. I've caught a lot of trout with it though. Some old-time anglers have taken pretty hefty bags of salmon with natural minnow, so I guess it's only the modern angler's terrific choice of baits that has caused it to fall out of favour. I was going to fish it hard last summer (1976), but with the drought conditions there weren't any fish to throw at!

There are times when a fresh, lively salmon will hammer into a bait with terrific enthusiasm, hooking itself solidly. They have smashed into floats when I have been retrieving them along the surface on days when I've been coarse fishing. Such suicidal fish are rare unfortunately, but knowing they will sometimes have a go at a surface bait wound up-stream, did give me the idea of trotting a spinner to a difficult lie and retrieving slowly back. I have caught one or two fish like this. One was caught where the high but sloping bank made the angler very obviously visible when he cast to fish, so a spinner was trotted, retrieved, a good fish took and was landed. Another angler, seeing the float from a distance, thought the fish was caught on worm. I didn't enlighten him.

But back to this hooking business. Remember that when spinning, the length of line is ever-changing, and should you strike, you must strike damned hard on a long line, but a lot less hard on a short one; the latter specially when fishing lighter tackle in low water conditions. And don't fish with the rod pointing down the line, or a really hard take can then cause tackle failure.

Things to be wary of when a salmon is hooked is head-shaking for one. It thumps the rod like hell, can loosen the hook hold, and frightens me to death if it's a big fish. I always ease pressure when this happens, the fish usually stops and then goes off on a long run. Another time the hook-hold may give, is when a fish explodes from the water, but as this is usually the termination of a run the angler is not holding it hard anyway, so there's little can be done — unless one believes in the power of prayer.

Playing a salmon

Whether or not Barrie and Ken wish me to write about playing the fish I don't know, but it's not much good solidly hooking the thing if you don't get it onto the bank.

A salmon is often a big fish. It is also a strong fish, a fast fish, an acrobatic fish, and a fish that often likes to move around relieving the angler of a lot of line in the process. And this last is one thing that novice anglers don't really appreciate; that it is always best to keep a fish on as short a line as possible. If a fish takes off downstream — get off after it. If it takes off up-stream — get off after it. The more line you lose from the reel, the longer it will take to get the fish back into a controllable position.

Now I don't mean by that last remark that if a big fish takes off you should hang on hard — that's the last thing you should do even with heavy tackle, for either the hook will tear out or break, or the line will break, or something disastrous will happen. What you should do is chase it upstream or down, letting as little line off the reel as you can, and retrieving as you near the animal. With a fish that's run downstream, pass it by and get below it, for you should try and play a big fish from downstream of it.

The foregoing is fine for clear banks, but what of obstructed banks? Sometimes the obstructions can be traversed, trees can be passed by taking the rod around; the river may be shallow enough to wade round

58 Dave Steuart tails a salmon caught spinning with his 'toy reel'.

and, if you have a companion, marvels can be accomplished. All this is necessary when a fish runs down, but not so if a fish goes up, as (unless it goes around a bend) the angler can usually get the fish back from below, since the fish is fighting both current and angler. If the bank is clear, however, as I said in the beginning, get off after it!

What if a big fish has gone a long way down and the obstructions are impassable? You can try pumping it up if you are restricted in either direction, but if the bank upstream is open, walk the fish up. When the fish has finished its downward rush and turned to face the current, wind tight, clamp your hand upon the reel drum and walk upriver. The fish will usually come up with you without fuss so long as you keep the pressure steady. Walk it up as far as you think necessary, or as far as you can go, then walk down retrieving line until you are opposite the fish or have to repeat the procedure. The fish may go down again and you may have to go 'walkies' a lot before eventually winning the day.

The first thing I do if I hook a salmon of any size upstream of a bridge, sluice, obstructed bank, or anywhere that I cannot follow down, is walk it up well away from trouble if it is at all feasible. I feel a lot happier and in a much more masterful position once I've done that.

If a fish has gone down and you cannot get it back, there are still a few courses open. You can let all the line from the reel and send a companion down to try and cast across it. If he is successful, cut your line, go down and re-tie. If you are on your own and possess a spare reel or spool of line, you can let off the line, tie it to a tree, go down with the rod and reel fitted with the spare line, cast and pick up your original line, try and gain some slack, then cut and tie to the new stuff. You can look for a largish tree branch (not waterlogged), tie your line to it, chuck it well out, and hope to pick it up below with the fish still attached — or you can go swimming. Rather you than me.

Salmon play pretty fair as a rule. They don't dive into weeds and snags, unless they are stale fish that have learnt the area. One place I fished last season, where because of the low water the few fish became potted, they used to disappear during the day beneath an old turbine house in dead slack water. When they came out in the evening, a fish hooked would belt straight back underneath.

Anglers will always argue amiably. When using a fixed spool reel, Barrie recommends back-pedalling to a running fish, but I disagree. It may be adequate to play some fish this way, but I personally don't like it for fast-moving fish like game fish, or when fishing with very fine lines. The reels are not balanced to revolve fast through the gears and one gets a 'rock' action when a fish is bolting. I admit that to play a fish from the clutch it is essential to have a reel with an ultra-smooth clutch, with no high spots, but there are such models and regular servicing to keep them so is entirely up to the angler.

After a big fish has been landed that has taken a lot of line, remove the terminal tackle and let the loose line flow freely downstream from the spool. This will remove the kinks put in the line by the drum revolving as the fish ran. It is a good idea to do this on any reel occasionally, for the line well down a spool will get crimped by the line pressure above.

Tackle

As we have just talked of fixed spool reels I will mention reels before rods.

There are only two types worth bothering with when salmon spinning, and they are the fixed spool reel and the multiplier. I occasionally

59 Removing a treble that was very well home.

spin with a centre pin, but that is just the whim of a fool: the other two types are far more efficient for the job. If you are only interested in purchasing one model, buy a large fixed spool reel, but if you are going to fish the season through you will require two models; as a comparison, a Mitchell 300 and a Mitchell 306 or their equivalents.

For big fish, an open river, and heavy lines, the multiplier is nicer to use and is my choice, and *is* easy to cast with despite the talk of overruns. But it is easier to cast with a fixed spool reel in awkward places, in rocky, tree-lined rivers. Where following is not possible, heavy tackle is necessary even if the fish are not over-large. In these sorts of rivers, as mentioned previously, it is essential to be able to place a bait into little holes between branches, under foliage and so on. A reel needs to carry at least 100 yards of 15-20 lb breaking strain for these conditions, and I would prefer it to carry 150-200 yards.

For the open river with runs of big fish, a reel that will hold the same sort of lengths and breaking strains is ideal.

For summer, and upstream work, when a river is less strong, when the fish are smaller, where I am casting light baits, and where I have no fear of losses, a Mitchell 300 or equivalent, loaded with 8-12 lb b.s. is ample. I often fish very much lighter than that, only half the recommended b.s., but 10 lb b.s. is what I would recommend for summer salmon — only lighter stuff if I knew the angler's capabilities.

With big fish like salmon I work out first what line strength is sensible to give me a fair chance of success and, along with other factors, a rod (and reel) is dictated by that. For heavy lines on the big river, a double-handed 10-foot job would be fine, but too awkward on a little river where a single-handed, strong, 8- or 9-footer, capable of handling the same line strength, would be a better proposition. For summer work a medium action 8- or 9-footer, coupled to the 10 lb line, gives an angler a deal of fun. Salmon are often full of fight in the warmer water and create hell — and heaven — for the angler!

I don't apologise for not giving the reader of this chapter much information on the multitude of spinning baits available, and their uses. I consider it more important that he or she know something about the fish, and its behaviour to the size of bait and the manner in which it is fished at different times of year. As yet there is no infallible spinning bait, and if I *had* found one, I wouldn't tell you!

60 Being hard.

SEA TROUT

Much of the information given in Fred J. Taylor's chapter on 'Spinning for Trout' (see page 137) will apply equally to the catching of sea trout, and so it will be pointless to repeat it all here. Rather will I confine myself to just a couple of things that he is unlikely to have touched upon; the variation between the sea trout's habits and those of its brown trout cousins(?).

Sea trout are the shyest fish I know, much shyer than brown trout or even chub, but unlike chub they are also extremely tackle-shy. This is surprising when one considers that the fish may never have seen tackle of any sort, and is not basing this caution on experience. As an illustration of the sea trout's shyness, I will quote a time when I was feeding maggots to a sea trout of some 8 lb in the River Avon at Christchurch. The fish greedily came up and took each one I threw in, and I thought it was going to be easy to catch. A couple of maggots on a 12 was refused, as they were on a 14: a single maggot freelined on size 16 to 2 lb was looked at several times but refused also, while all the time the fish took loose offerings. I had no hooks smaller, so gave the fish best.

A brown trout or a rainbow would have taken straight away. Even browns that I have caught and returned would be re-caught when fished with tackle as light as a 16 to 2 lb.

Having established the shyness of sea trout, spinning for them is far more profitable on dull days, or in water fining down after a flood, when fresh fish (which are better takers anyway) are liable to be in the river.

It doesn't matter how high the river remains; providing the dirt has left it but there is still some colour tinge, sea trout will take a spinner reasonably well in these conditions during daylight hours.

Metal devons, blue and silver about $1\frac{1}{2}$-inch and Mepp type sizes 2 and 3 have caught me plenty of sea trout in high water, and I have taken a number of fish on 2-inch devons and Mepp size 4 in very coloured water, over gravel shallows that are usually exposed when the water recedes. Obviously one would be foolish to fish with line lighter than 6 or 7 lb b.s. in heavy water, when the sea trout might be 6-pounders or more.

It is when the river is running normal and clear that sea trout show a difference to browns. Dependent upon the river's stock, huge fish, maybe in the teens of pounds, will show a preference for a tiny spoon, size 0, or a little gold or silver devon only $\frac{3}{4}$-inch or 1-inch long. And it is often essential to fish it on extremely fine tackle. Most of the very big browns I read about are taken on pretty substantial baits.

Although I have taken sea trout in a number of river with devons, I have generally done better with bar-spoons.

Upstream spinning can be just as successful for sea trout as for salmon, sometimes extremely fast winding bringing the best results.

For fishing very fine I have a spinning rod made from fly blanks, that allows me to fish extremely fine lines without fear of breaks — except through my own fault or caused by unknown snags. It was originally made for mullet spinning, which fish is also shy of coarse lines at times.

I would like to make one final observation. With such a difficult customer as a sea trout, best results will probably come by fly fishing at night, unless one wishes and is permitted to fish with worm or maggot.

References

BATES, L. V., *Sporting Tactics for Coarse Fish* Herbert Jenkins 1962

BICKERDYKE, J., *Angling for Pike* Ch.4. Thorson Publishers 1959

BULLER, F., *Pike* Part 3 Sections 6-14. Macdonald 1971

FALKUS, H. and BULLER, F., *Freshwater Fishing* Ch.41 & 42. Macdonald 1975

GAMMON, C., *Hook, Line and Spinner* Heinemann 1959

GAY, M., *Beginner's Guide to Pike Fishing* Ch.9. Pelham Books 1975

GIBBINSON, J., *Pike* Osprey Publishing Ltd. 1974

HAMPTON, J. F., *Hampton on Pike Fishing* Ch.3. Chambers 1947

JARDINE, A., *Pike and perch* Ch.4. Routledge 1896

KEAL, W., *Bill Keal's Book of Fishing* Clipper Press 1972

LONSDALE LIBRARY *Fine Angling for Coarse Fish* Ch.18. Seeley Service 1930

MARSHALL-HARDY, E., *Angling Ways* Ch.30-33. Barrie and Jenkins 1973 (10th edn)

MAUNSELL, G. W., *Fisherman's Vade Mecum* A & C Black 1933

RICKARDS, R. B., *Catch More Perch* Ch.5. Wolfe Pbg Co. 1974

RICKARDS, R. B., *Pike Fishing Step by Step* Cassell 1976

RICKARDS, R. B., and WHITEHEAD, K., *Plugs and plug fishing* A & C Black 1976

SPENCER, S., *Pike on the Plug* H. F. & G. Witherby 1936

WANLESS, A., *The Science of Spinning for salmon and trout* Herbert Jenkins 1930

WANLESS, A., *Thread-line Questions Answered* Herbert Jenkins 1933

WEBB, R. and RICKARDS, R. B., *Fishing for Big Pike* Ch.6. A & C Black 1976 (2nd edn)

Appendix

Detailed illustrations are shown on the following pages

SPINNERS, SPOONS & BAITS

TACKLE

(including 'business-end' tackle)